CHASING ROOTS

Chasing Roots

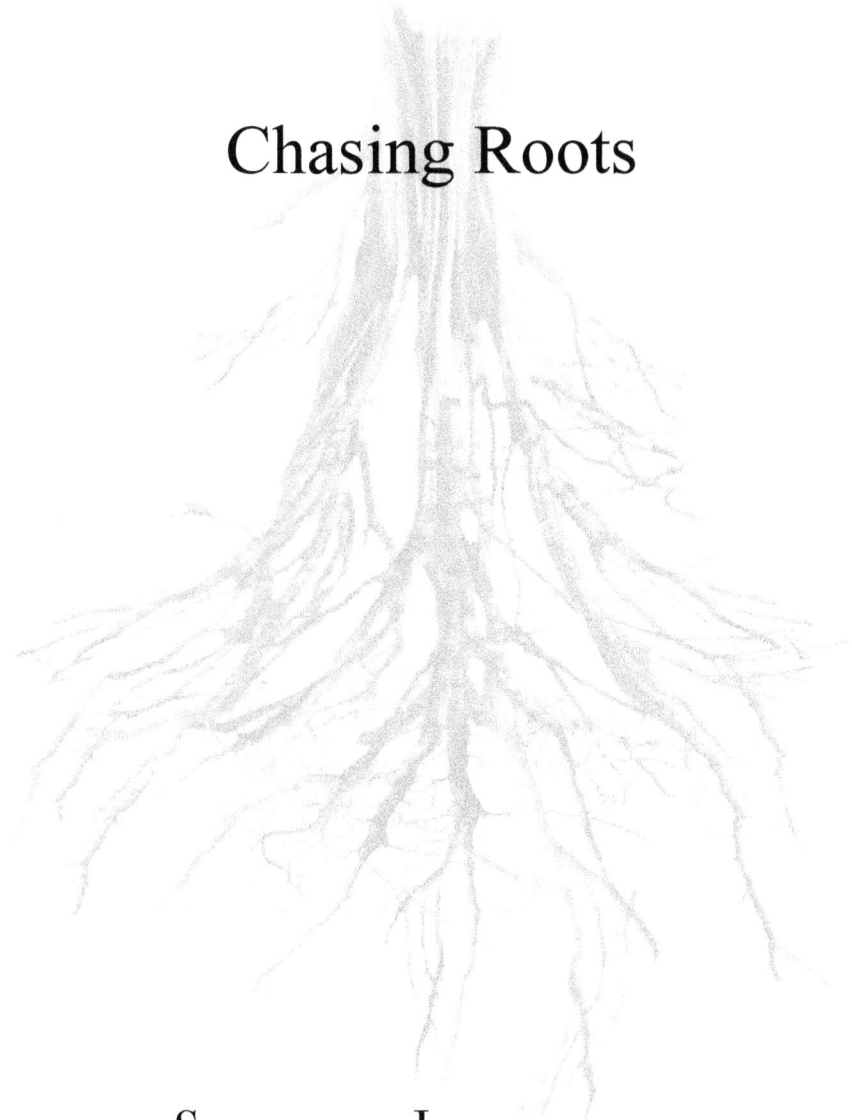

SHALANDOR JOHNSON 2021

TO REQUEST PERMISSION, CONTACT THE PUBLISHER AT:
JOHNSONSPROGRESS@GMAIL.COM

FIRST PRINTING: 2021

Paperback: ISBN 978-0-578-98710-1

JohnsonTrax Productions & Publishing, LLC
Houston, MS 38851
WWW.UNFINISHEDCLAY.ORG

NOTE: ALL SCRIPTURE REFERENCES ARE TAKEN FROM THE HOLY BIBLE KJV

CHASING ROOTS

IN LOVING MEMORY OF MY FATHER

Rev. David Reel Jr. February 9, 1928 – April 14, 1984

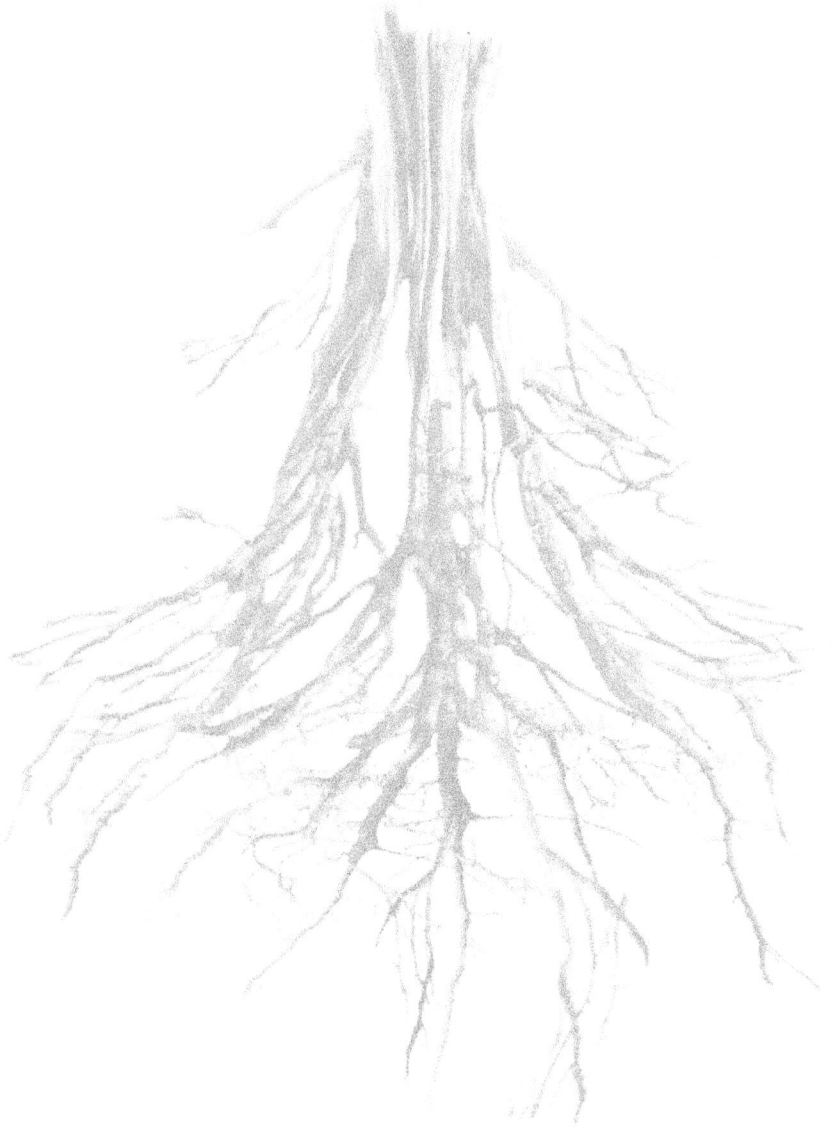

Dear Daddy,

Thank you for being the best dad ever for four years to me. Even though I was a little girl, I remember your eyes and how you would look under at me and smile. I remember your strong stature and stance. You were stern but loving. Your heart was full of love, and in hindsight, I understand that some of the love that I received was manifested prayers and fruit that proved you had grown and changed into a better man. You were not a perfect man, but you were perfect for me. For that, I thank you! Your seeds are thriving in the earth, and your purpose lives on through your children. Daddy, I even forget songs and hum the tunes to play it off like it was on purpose just like you! You were amazing in my eyes, and I can hardly wait to see your smile again in Heaven. Love you much!

Your Baby Girl,

Shalandor Reel- Johnson

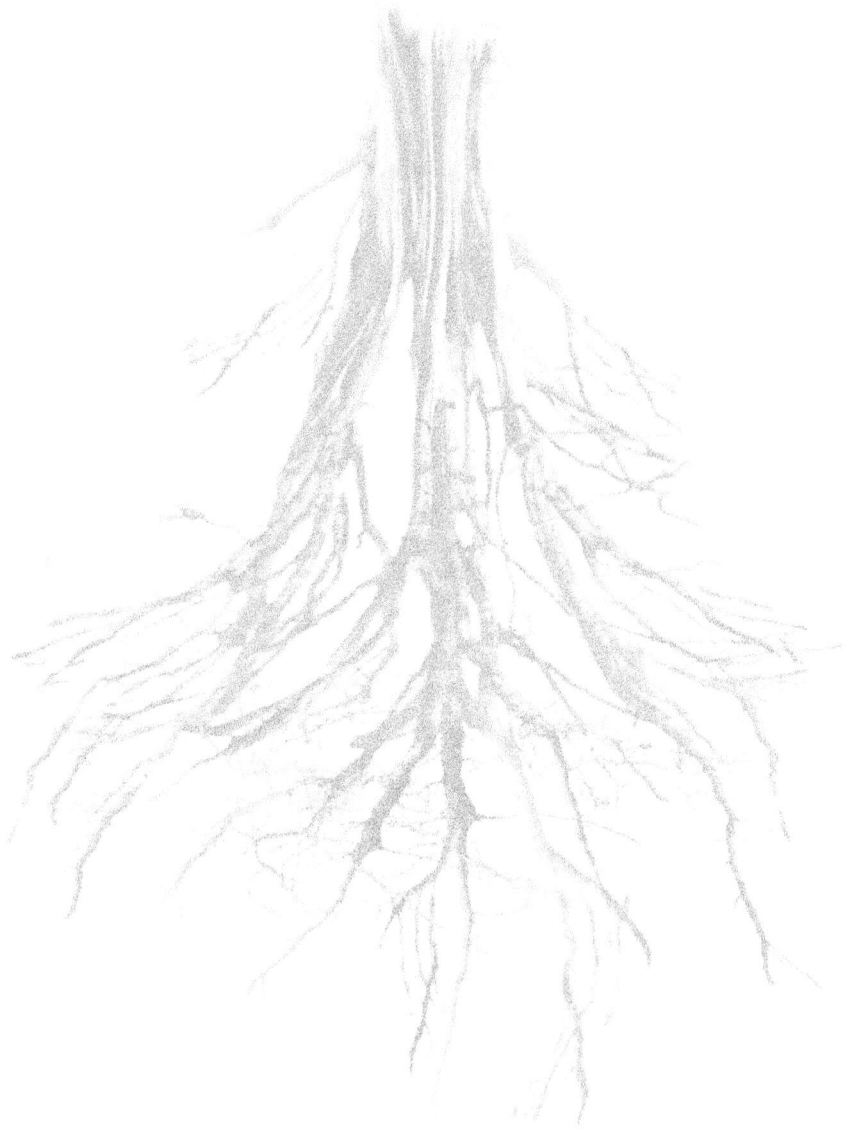

Special Thanks

I would like to take this opportunity to thank each and every one of you for your love and support. To my wonderful husband and Pastor, Stan Johnson. You are absolutely a Godsend, and I am grateful that you chose me to do this thing called life with! I am grateful for your unbiased love and wise counsel daily! You've walked with me, and we have overcome many obstacles together. Thank you for 20 blessed years of marriage, and I look forward to many more with you!

To my sweet children Kirk, Kirklyn, and LaSarah. Momma loves you beyond words. You three are the drive I need every day and the reasons why I refuse to settle for ordinary. I dream and take leaps of faith not because I'm brave, but because I want to create a pattern and habit so that you can dream without excuse. Go for what you know in life and refuse to settle. Greatness is in each of you equally!

To my siblings: We started out as ten, but now we are eight strong. I thank God for the seed that binds us close together. Whether near or far, nothing can separate me from loving you! I pray that God continues to grant each of you your heart's desire.

To the select ladies that I call friends! Thank you for being there for me even when I was not consistent. I've had many changes over the years, but you all have stood by my side. For that I say thank you!

Brittney Reel! Thank you for listening to God and allowing him to push you further into your assignments and gifts. You have been the perfect help and encourager. Thank you so much for editorial services and just being a listening ear when I needed it the most!

Last, but certainly not least, a big THANK YOU to all of my encouragers and supporters far and near. You are why I keep on keeping on. I say all of the time that I understand that I'm not assigned to everyone, but I sure do love those that God has placed in my midst! I love you all!

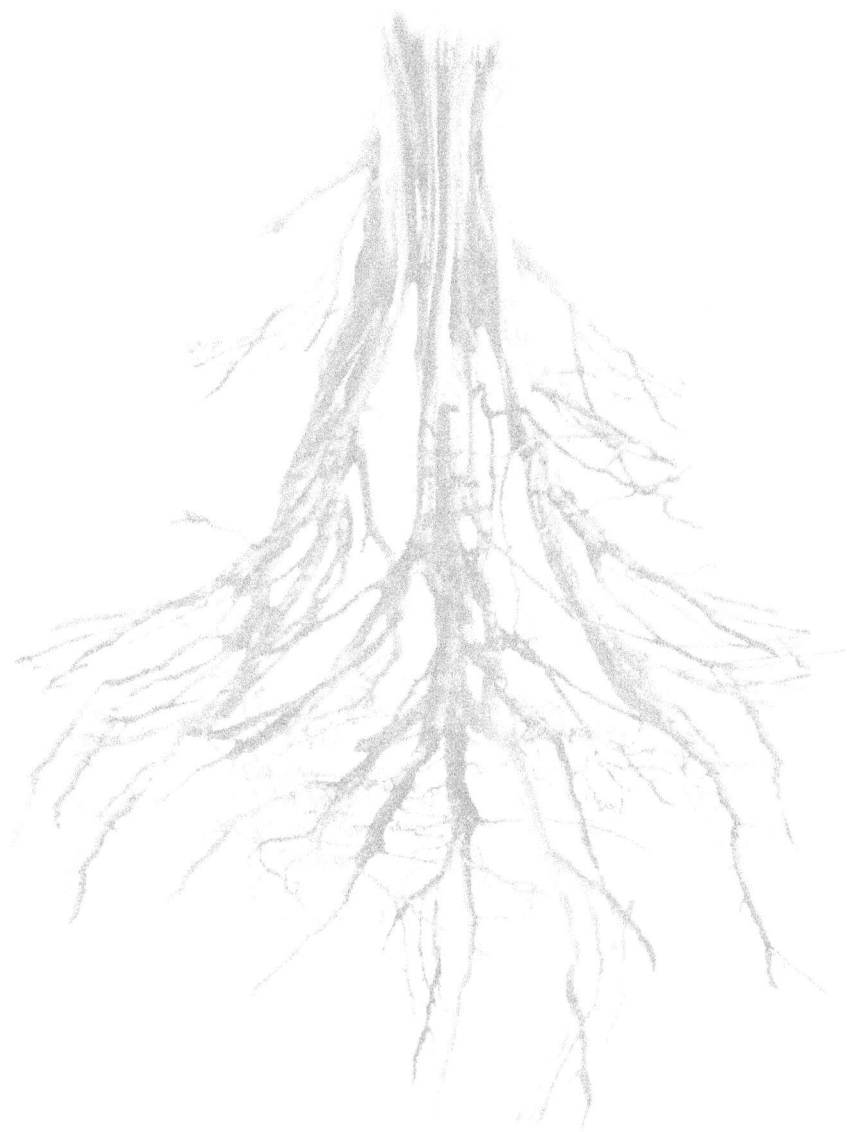

Table of Contents

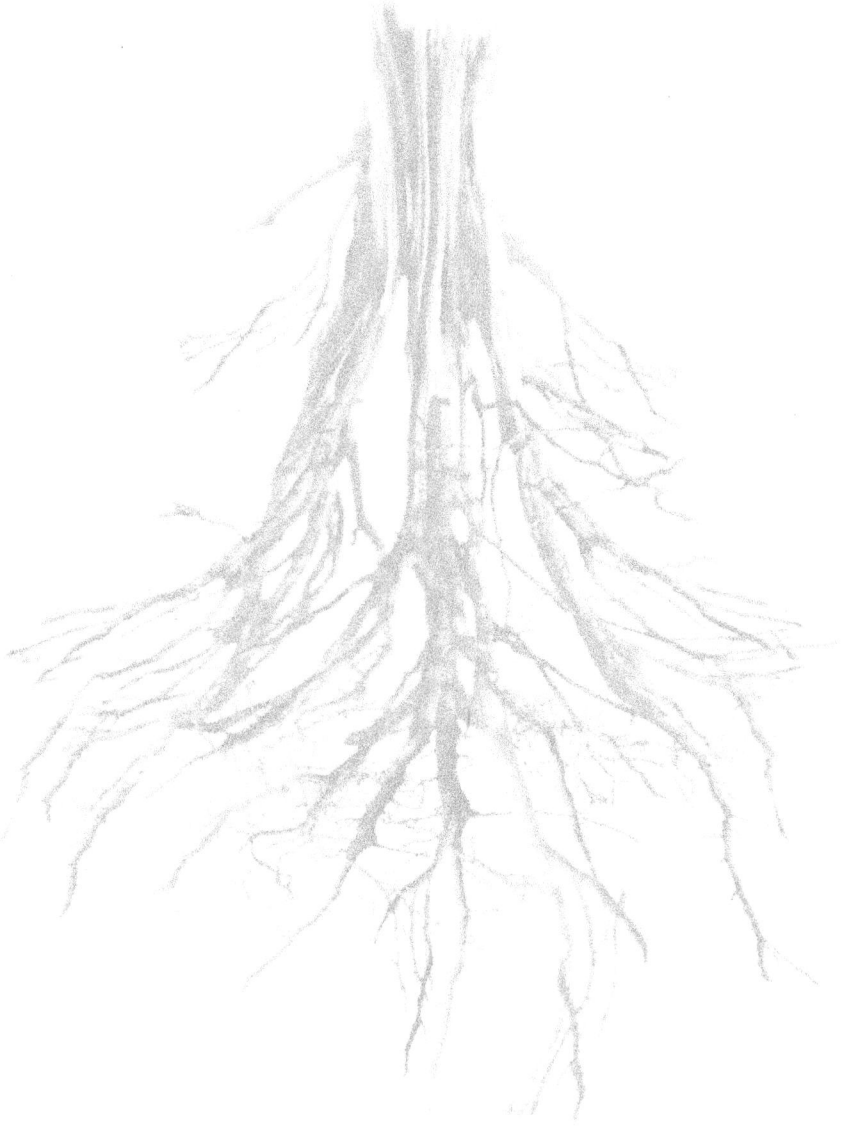

Foreword by Pastor Stan Johnson

How did I get here? Who am I? What is my purpose? These are just some of the questions we may ask during our lifetime. Life can bring great victories, but it can also be confusing at times, and we can feel like we are defeated. Especially if we are not rooted in Christ. It is good to do a self-examination on why we act and react the way we do, and this book is an excellent read on how to do just that.

Evangelist Shae Johnson teaches us how to dig deep to find root causes of our behaviors in this wonderfully written book. Her transparency in her own life teaches us to be honest about ourselves in ways we haven't been before. Follow her on her journey as you simultaneously embark on your own path to discover areas that need fine tuning in order to progress further in your purpose. Embrace this difficult but necessary journey with her as she chases roots. You'll definitely appreciate it after it's done.

Pastor Stan K. Johnson, Author of Night Vision

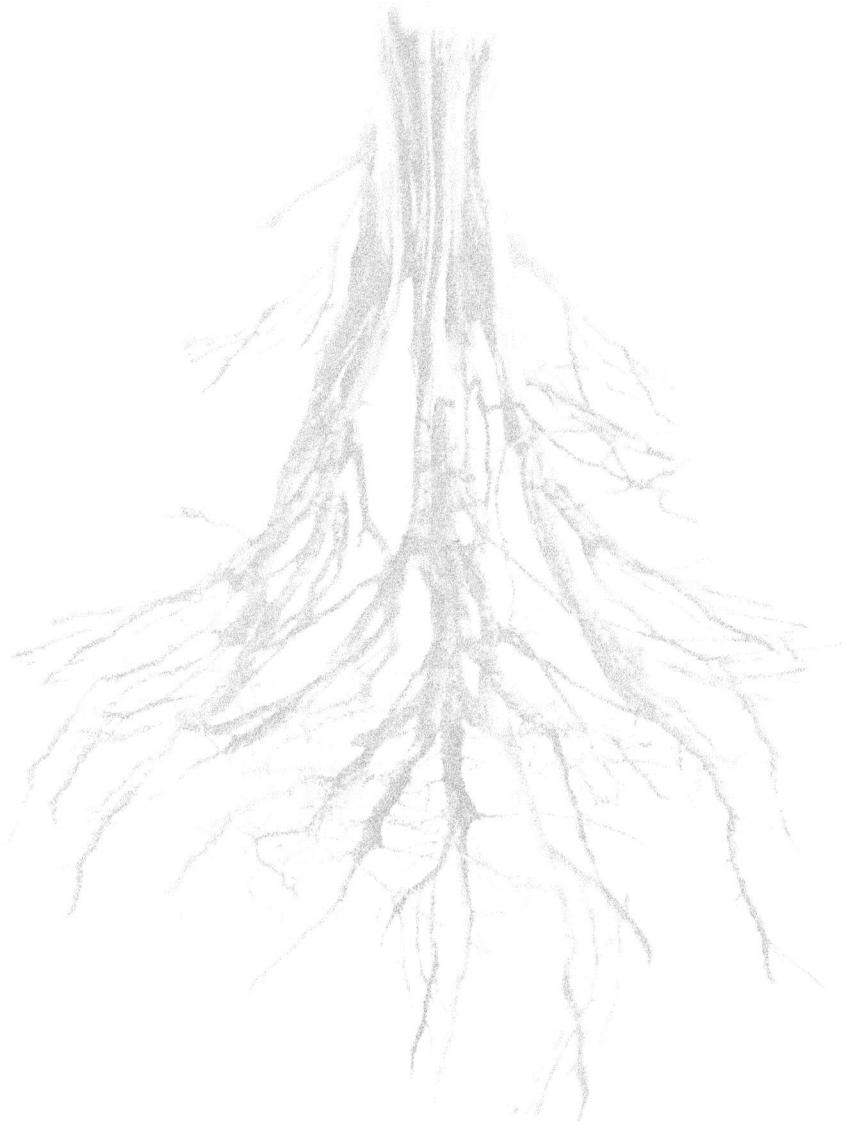

DEAR FRIEND,

THANK YOU FOR PURCHASING THIS BOOK. I WANT YOU TO KNOW THAT I POURED MY HEART INTO THE PAGES. I WANT TO GIVE SUGGESTIONS ON HOW TO UTILIZE THE CONTENT IN THE PAGES TO FOLLOW. THERE IS A DEVOTIONAL AND STUDY AT THE END OF EVERY CHAPTER. PLEASE BE AWARE THAT THERE ARE QUESTIONS EMBEDDED WITHIN THE CHAPTER TEXTS AS WELL. ANYTIME YOU COME UPON A SECTION OR A QUESTION, PLEASE TAKE A MOMENT TO HIGHLIGHT THE QUESTIONS AND RETURN TO ANSWER THEM TRUTHFULLY. I HIGHLY SUGGEST THAT YOU HAVE A SEPARATE NOTEBOOK OR JOURNAL AND HIGHLIGHTER AVAILABLE AS YOU READ. MAKE NOTES OF ANYTHING THAT STANDS OUT OR CATCHES YOUR ATTENTION. DO NOT RUSH THROUGH THE TEXTS.

DISCLAIMER THIS BOOK DOES NOT SERVE AS OR REPLACE PROFESSIONAL COUNSELING SESSIONS. IF YOU FEEL THE NEED TO SEEK COUNSELING, PLEASE DO SO AT YOUR DISCRETION.

LASTLY, AFTER YOU READ THIS BOOK PLEASE REVIEW OR SHARE YOUR THOUGHTS WITH ME VIA SOCIAL MEDIA, EMAIL, OR MESSENGER. I'D LOVE TO HEAR YOUR FEEDBACK. REFER THIS BOOK TO YOUR FAMILY, CHURCHES, AND FRIENDS IF YOU FEEL IT IS A BENEFICIAL GROUP STUDY! I'M EXCITED ABOUT OUR JOURNEY TOGETHER! ARE YOU READY TO CHASE ROOTS? OK, READY, SET, LET'S GO!

LOVE YOU MUCH,

SHAE

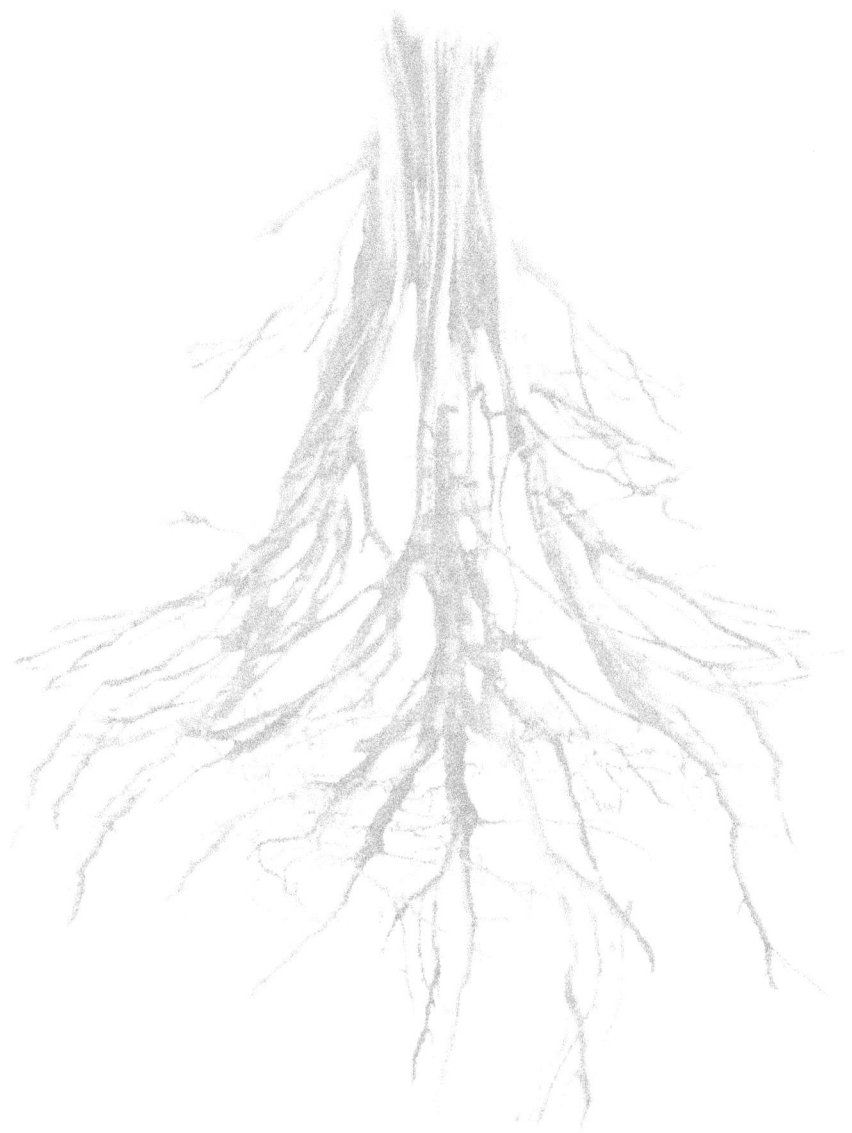

<u>Introduction</u>

I can remember in 1994 when the classic movie "The Lion King'' came to theaters. I was a teenager approximately fifteen years of age. There was this one specific scene where Simba, the young lion cub and son of the slain Lion King Mufasa, was on the run and was found hiding in a foreign land. Graphiki, the Kingdom's spiritual guide, found Simba and urged him to follow him down to a brook. When Simba arrived at the brook, they had a quick yet powerful dialogue. Graphiki asked the confused young lion cub the question, "Do you know who you are?" Simba stated in response, "I don't know who I am!" Graphiki smiled big and threw his monkey paws on the cub's shoulder and stated, "But I KNOW who you are," and he pointed down at the brook. When Simba looked at his reflection in the water, he first saw himself as is, but the wise monkey then pointed for him to stare harder. As he looked closer, he no longer saw himself, but he was now gazing eye to eye with the reflection of his father. His father spoke to him via the spirit and stated, "Simba, you have forgotten me? REMEMBER WHO YOU ARE!"

I can remember that one scene sending me into an array of emotions. Something hit me in the pit of my stomach that night. It wasn't the quickening of the Holy Ghost either. IT WAS FEAR! Simply because I was functioning but not thriving. I didn't know "who I was," and I found myself admitting that I was fresh in an identity crisis.

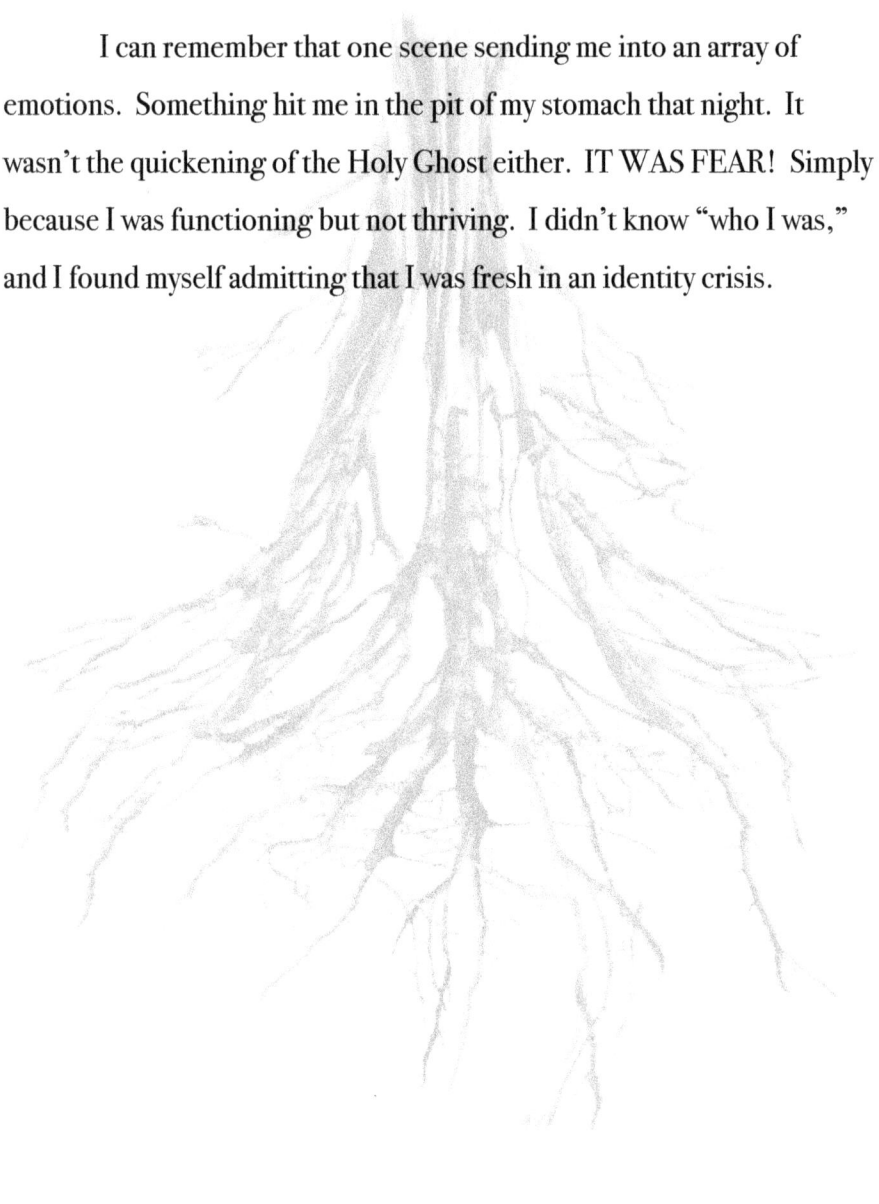

Chapter 1

<u>The Facts</u>

You may be wondering why I would proclaim that I was experiencing an identity crisis. I can hear you even now stating, "Now, you KNOW you are Sarah Mae Reel and Dave Reel Jr's baby daughter, "The Reels" aka "those singing folks." If that crossed your mind, then I would agree and verify that your thoughts are clear! Those descriptions are all correct, but what is not known are my fraternal roots. My mother's lineage can successfully be traced at least 5 generations back. My father's side is more complicated. I am specifically referring to my father's father. I know my dad, and I have a picture of his dad. That is as far as I can go. Since there is very little information that I can verify, a void exists in that area of my life. The very fact that I cannot pen my father's lineage (the seed carriers) bothers me tremendously. I will go deeper to explain my emotional turmoil.

Lineage is important to God, and if you are a student of the Bible or even pick up a bible occasionally, that's something that will become apparent even in the first few chapters of the first book. Biblical generational lineage teaches us many things. God begins to reveal in Genesis the history of mankind, and He gives names. He lets us know that the human root begins in the Garden of Eden by way of his creation of Adam and then his help meet Eve. Now, follow me if you will. After Adam and Eve jacked up the good life and sinned, they were given the command to be fruitful and multiply. BAM! Shortly after, we are given the first family lineage of the bible and human history. You will read where Adam begat Cain and Abel. After Cain killed Abel, Eve birthed another son named Seth. In the chapters and books to follow you will find all kinds of names and family lineages, and it became apparent to me that the purposeful recordkeeping of God showed major truths throughout biblical history. One truth I observed is that who you are right now, your entire genetic makeup, was passed to you from past generations. You can literally contribute your thought process, humor, personality, physical traits, and habits (good and bad) to a previous seed in your family genetic garden.

Now listen, there are two spiritual beings that are well aware of your presence and authority in the Earth, and I'm referring to God and Satan. God created you, but Satan studies you! Let that sink in! God, our creator, knows exactly who he created you to be, but Satan does not want you to come into the knowledge of your purpose. Therefore, he strategically plants traps and bad seeds in your bloodline to divert purpose and detour your destiny. He has done that since day one!

Consider how he derailed Adam and Eve (Genesis) in their perfect world! Satan understood Adam and Eve's purpose on earth even before they understood themselves. He purposely planted a seed of doubt and speculation when he questioned Eve about what God commanded, already knowing that God gave clear instructions from the beginning. That seed of speculation created a void right then and there that led to them wondering and asking the question "Is something missing that we should know about?" Later, you can find them getting out of the will of God and disobeying him by trying to fulfill the need to "know." Adam and Eve sinned and fell from grace while searching for answers. You will read where after they make the wrong decision, they find themselves naked, hiding, and in an identity crisis. They no longer knew their true identity! I'd like to stop right here and pose a question. Is it possible that people whom society deems as troublemakers, prostitutes, alcoholics, drug addicts, liars, cheaters, blasphemers, atheists and so forth are searching out voids and missing pieces of their identities but may not know how to articulate it? I don't claim to know a whole lot, but I do know that voids show up in the earth in various ways. We were created to have knowledge and awareness simply because we were created in the likeness and image of God. It is Satan that does not want us to understand our power in the earth. I have a quick question for you, and I need your honest answer. DO YOU KNOW WHO YOU ARE?

Let's pray and ask God for revelation.

Father, we come to you thanking you for life, health and strength. Lord, we ask that you speak to our hearts as we begin to search for real answers. Help us to understand that our life's purpose and plan was designed by you! If anyone is struggling with their identity, shed knowledge according to your wisdom and power to them right now! We trust you with the journey! IN JESUS'S NAME WE PRAY, AMEN!

CHAPTER STUDY SECTION

Chapter 1: The Facts

LET US LOOK AT THE LIFE OF THE APOSTLE PAUL. HE ADHERED TO THE LAW THE BEST THAT HE COULD. HE HAD INCREDIBLE CREDENTIALS. HE WAS CIRCUMCISED THE EIGHTH DAY (LEVITICUS 12:3), HAD A PURE JEWISH HERITAGE OF THE TRIBE OF BENJAMIN, A HEBREW OF HEBREWS, AND A ZEALOUS PHARISEE WHO WAS TAUGHT BY THE MOST RESPECTED RABBI OF THE DAY NAMED GAMALIEL. WHAT A RESUME! WITH ALL OF THESE ACCOLADES, HE DID NOT KNOW WHO HE WAS UNTIL HE HAD AN ENCOUNTER WITH JESUS (ACTS 9:1-9). WE CAN SPEND A GOOD PART OF OUR LIVES THINKING WE HAVE IT TOGETHER, BUT IF JESUS IS NOT THE HEAD OF OUR LIVES, ALL OTHER THINGS ARE COUNTED AS LOSSES (PHILIPPIANS 3: 4-8).

HAVE YOU EVER FOUND YOURSELF IN AN IDENTITY CRISIS OR FEELING LIKE YOU WERE NOT LIVING UP TO YOUR FULL POTENTIAL?

WHAT ARE SOME OF THE THINGS YOU ARE PASSIONATE TOWARDS?

WHAT ARE YOUR LIKES AND DISLIKES?

WHAT ARE SOME OF YOUR CHILDHOOD EXPERIENCES (GOOD AND BAD)?

Root Nourishment

WHEN YOU BECOME A BORN-AGAIN BELIEVER AND ENTER INTO THE REVELATION OF JESUS BEING THE SON OF GOD WITH ALL POWER (MATT. 16:16), THEN YOUR LIFE CAN OPERATE IN THE PROPER WAY OF GLORIFYING GOD. YOUR IDENTITY IS FOUND WITHIN CHRIST AND HIS REDEMPTION PLAN.

21

Chapter Notes and Thoughts

Chapter 2

<u>On The Run</u>

Whenever you are unsure of your identity and who you truly are, it becomes a breeding ground for satanic interruptions. I call it the battle of the sowers. Voids excrete a spiritual aroma to the enemy, sort of like the attraction and chemistry between lovers. There's just this "thing" present that screams "Satisfy me!" Voids desire satisfaction as well as gratification, even if the effects are temporary. Sometimes a person is aware of this fact, and sometimes people are clueless. It just depends on the level of maturity and spiritual awareness one has in order to know that there is such a thing present in their life. I haven't always had the spiritual knowledge that I possess now, but I can honestly say that I had the spiritual aroma that signified I had a void. It wasn't a physical scent; it was a physical pull. The older people describe it as a flesh appetite and boy did I have a big one.

My void began when my dad died in 1984. I was only four years old at the time, and I remember my daddy vividly. Baby, when I say that he had spoiled me rotten I mean it to the twenty-fifth power. I can see why he was so proud though, because I was the child of his old age.

Momma was forty-five and he was fifty-one when I was born. I consider myself the grand finale of the Reel clan. The last child born of ten. He died from Leukemia. I didn't understand. What was this Leukemia and cancer talk anyway? All I know is that when he died, I felt different. I couldn't describe it. I had so many questions. Where did daddy go? WHY did he have to go? Why was momma looking worried? Why were my siblings crying? Question after question filled my head, but I had no answers in my heart. My life changed that day in April of 1984. It was something missing in my life and that is where I picked up the spiritual aroma of a void. It made me crave attention, and I was too young to understand the reason why. All I knew was that my flesh craved something that was missing for the first time. I needed my daddy, but the void interpreted it as "you need the love of a man." As I grew, it grew. It let off the aroma in the form of my actions. It screamed "fill me."

For many years I had no clue, but now I know that it was there. I can't be a help to you without first admitting that I needed the help myself. So many times, we inherit or formulate coping mechanisms that are toxic to our lives. What do you do when life gets hard? What's your default emotion? Do you cry? Do you withdraw or retreat? Do you become angry or depressed? We all cope with stress and trauma differently. Here is my hope, though. I hope and pray that if you tend to run, you run to the right source. I've learned that "running" isn't really the issue or a bad thing. Actually, we were created to need a rescuer.

When life gets hard, we need someone stronger to help us. If you feel the need to run and hide, that's fine but can I suggest that you find refuge and shelter in God the father? He is who we should turn to and honestly that's not many people's first choice. Why? People choose God last because our flesh wars against the things of the spirit. It actually hurts to say, "That bothered me." We are taught at young ages to be tough, but now I know that I'm not required to be tough, I'm required to be a daughter of the King and HE is tough. He is our defense team all by himself. HE causes our enemies to be at peace with us. HE upholds us with his right arm and hides us under the shadow of his wings! HE lends that power to us when we link up with him. HE gives US power to root out things that are not like him and HE ALWAYS causes us to win! Why won't you once and for all kill the minor things that are trying to kill you? It's been way too long already! Get up! It's time for you to chase the thing that has been silently chasing you! What are you waiting for? Your freedom is at stake. It's ok to run, you just have to know who to run to!

Let's pray about it! *Abba Father, we run to you! We need your mercy! Command your warring angels to come and fight alongside us as we confront the things that we have been chasing in our minds and hearts. We are sick of the tormentors. We are sick of Satan's abuse. We no longer desire to live beneath our privilege of being called your sons and daughters. We understand that within our flesh, no good thing dwells. We also understand that whenever we desire to do good, evil is present. Nevertheless, your power is stronger than any bands that the enemy desires to hold us with. Lord, we are running but now we are coming towards you! Meet us! In Jesus's name. Amen!*

CHAPTER STUDY SECTION

Chapter 2: On the Run

REMEMBER GIDEON? HE IS THE ONE WHO DEFEATED THE MIDIANITES WHO WERE STRONGLY OPPOSING ISRAEL. HE STARTED WITH 32,000 PEOPLE, BUT THE LORD TRIMMED HIS ARMY TO ONLY 300. THAT IS HIS GLORY, BUT DO YOU KNOW THE REAL BACKDROP OF HIS STORY? BEFORE HE WON THIS VICTORY ISRAEL WAS SORE AFRAID AND BEGGING GOD FOR A LEADER. THE ANGEL OF THE LORD FOUND GIDEON SITTING UNDER AN OAK TREE THRESHING WHEAT SO THAT HIS PEOPLE COULD HAVE FOOD. HE IS HIDING AND FEARFUL BECAUSE OF THE MIDIANITES. GIDEON WAS THE ANSWER TO ISRAEL'S PRAYERS, BUT HE WAS ON THE RUN HIDING FOR HIS LIFE. GOD CALLS HIM A MIGHTY MAN OF VALOR EVEN IN HIS FEARFUL STATE. THE NAME HE RECEIVED DID NOT MATCH HIS CURRENT EMOTIONAL LOCATION, BUT GOD HAS A WAY OF CALLING THOSE THINGS THAT BE NOT AS THOUGH THEY WERE (ROMANS 4:17) GIDEON HAD AN ASSIGNMENT OVER HIS LIFE. JUST LIKE GIDEON, LIFE CAN HAVE US ON THE RUN, BUT IT WOULD BE BENEFICIAL TO STOP RUNNING AND LISTEN FOR THE VOICE OF GOD IN OUR LIVES. HE KNOWS OUR NAME EVEN WHEN WE ARE RUNNING THE OTHER WAY.

LIST THE THINGS IN YOUR LIFE THAT YOU HAVE NOT HAD THE COURAGE TO FACE.

Root Nourishment:

JUST AS GIDEON WAS THE ANSWER FOR ISRAEL'S VICTORY, PLEASE CONSIDER THAT MAYBE SOMEONE IS WAITING FOR YOU TO GIRD YOURSELF WITH STRENGTH. YOU JUST MAY BE THE KEY FOR SOMEONE ELSE'S VICTORY! STOP RUNNING.

Chapter Notes and Thoughts

Chapter 3

False Leads

False leads are birthed out of error and lies. To be honest, we all have had false leads in our lives. We all have traveled down roads and paths that seemed to have a dead end. Believe it or not, sometimes that's a blessing. It's better to understand and learn from an error or mistake in life than continue traveling down the road to nowhere wasting more time than necessary. Everyone's path is different, and no one person's life journey is the same. Even with that, one must understand that Satan, if given room, will try and re-route you as far away from your destiny as he possibly can! Thank God for saving grace! Now, I don't want you to think that this book is solely about "Satan and his plans." No, this book is about GOD coming through IN-SPITE of Satan and his little schemes. I already stated earlier that God created you, but Satan studies you! Why wouldn't you know how to understand the enemy's functions in order to beat him at his own game?

When referring to false leads, I'm describing the actions that we demonstrate in our flesh that draw our spirit away from God. Most times it is done through voids. For example, if a person feels as if they are being overlooked or ignored in life, they will in turn lead themselves down the road of becoming an attention seeker! You have a lot of individuals out here in the world that are living way lower than their destiny has purposed for them, yet they are chasing false leads. It's kind of like the young lady that shows all of her body to social media, or the young guy that is trying to impress his followers on Facebook insinuating that "the fast life" or "balling out" is actually a good thing! Here is what bothers me though. It's one thing for them to think their behaviors are okay, but you have the "false leads" under the comments encouraging and promoting this destructive thought process further! Please turn your spiritual hearing up and hear me well when I say this next statement. There is a thin line between judging and seeing that someone has a void that needs to be filled. It's all in how you view such individuals. They shouldn't be talked about; they should be prayed for. There is nothing more disturbing than seeing someone not living out their full potential. It can happen to anyone. Life has many people on the run following false leads (lies concerning who they are). The remedy for that is knowledge, support, and going to where that bad root lies. People must ask themselves when and where did this behavior start? You should inventory your past genetic family history and decide if the behavior is a common family trait.

I used to travel down a road of false leads, so I understand the tendency to do so. Mine started with searching for the love and adoration that I felt from my father. I can't fully articulate that longing, but I know that it caused me to seek love in the wrong places. Whatever my daddy said was the gospel to me, and I found myself lending that same trust and grace to others even though it wasn't earned. I was naive and green. So, if someone said I was ugly, guess what I thought of myself? Yep, I assumed I was ugly. It is also wise to understand that some bad seed sowers are not always strangers. As a matter of fact, I probably would've escaped half of the mental trauma I endured if that was solely the case. Unfortunately, the people who have the most influence in our lives are the people we trust. What has happened to you that has led you down paths of low-level thinking? You can dig up that root with the help of God our creator. If you don't mind, let's pray together right now.

Abba Father, we come to you as humble as we know how, thanking you for this moment in time. Father we thank you for your darling son, Jesus, who came so that we return back to our default identities of being sons and daughters of the most high. Father, allow us to feel your unwavering love as we come to terms with our lives. Many mistakes have been made along the way as well as many tears have been shed throughout this journey. We ask you now to remove any scales and blinders that may be hindering our lives and set us on Straight Street once again for your glory and namesake. Heal us EVERYWHERE we hurt!

We rebuke all lies and proclaim that the schemes and plots of the enemy are void and null in the mighty name of Jesus. Father we break any pledges, spiritual contracts, covenants, and promises that were verbally or emotionally made knowingly or unknowingly by fire in the Name of Jesus. We thank you that we see the light and live therein from this day forward. We declare that we are all that you say we are and nothing less. We walk hand in hand with Mercy and Grace daily. In Jesus's matchless name. Amen.

CHAPTER STUDY SECTION

Chapter 3: False Leads

FALSE LEADS WILL TAKE YOU DOWN A ROAD OF EMPTINESS. LET'S CONSIDER THIS LADY FOUND IN JOHN CHAPTER 4! YES, YOU KNOW HER, SHE IS THE "WOMAN AT THE WELL." WE'VE HEARD HER DISCUSSED OVER THE YEARS OVER THE PULPIT, IN SERMONS, POEMS, AND SUNDAY SCHOOL ILLUSTRATIONS. I'M SURE IF SHE WAS ALIVE TODAY, SHE'D BE FOUND SOMEWHERE PLEADING FOR US TO KEEP HER NAME OUT OF OUR MOUTHS! NEVERTHELESS, SHE IS UP FOR DISCUSSION ONCE AGAIN. MAY I HAVE A MOMENT TO OFFER HER A LITTLE GRACE? WE DISCUSS HER FRUIT (THIS WOMAN LOVED HER SOME MEN) BUT CAN WE TRACE HER ROOT? I WOULD SUGGEST THAT SOMEWHERE BEFORE SHE IS BROUGHT UP IN SCRIPTURE, SHE WAS CHASING FALSE LEADS! I BET SOME SLICK TALKING JOKER LIED TO HER AND MADE HER PROMISES THAT HE COULDN'T KEEP. OK, YOU'RE RIGHT, I CAN'T PROVE THAT STATEMENT BUT ONE THING FOR SURE IS THAT SHE HAD A VOID AND IT LET OFF THE SPIRITUAL AROMA THAT KEPT ATTRACTING PEOPLE THAT LEFT HER UNFULFILLED. I HAVE GOOD NEWS THOUGH. WHENEVER THERE IS PURPOSE WITHIN YOU, JESUS WILL COME AND VISIT YOU! SHE WENT FROM A WOMAN OF REPUTATION TO AN EVANGELIST WITHIN JUST ONE ENCOUNTER WITH THE RIGHT MAN! JESUS WAS THE MAN THAT MADE THE DIFFERENCE! HAVE YOU TALKED WITH HIM LATELY?

Root Nourishment: YOU HAVE A LEADER, AND HE (THE HOLY SPIRIT) WILL LEAD YOU IF YOU LET HIM! READ PROVERBS 3: 5-6. ACKNOWLEDGE HIM SO THAT HE CAN DIRECT YOUR PATH!

Chapter Notes and Thoughts

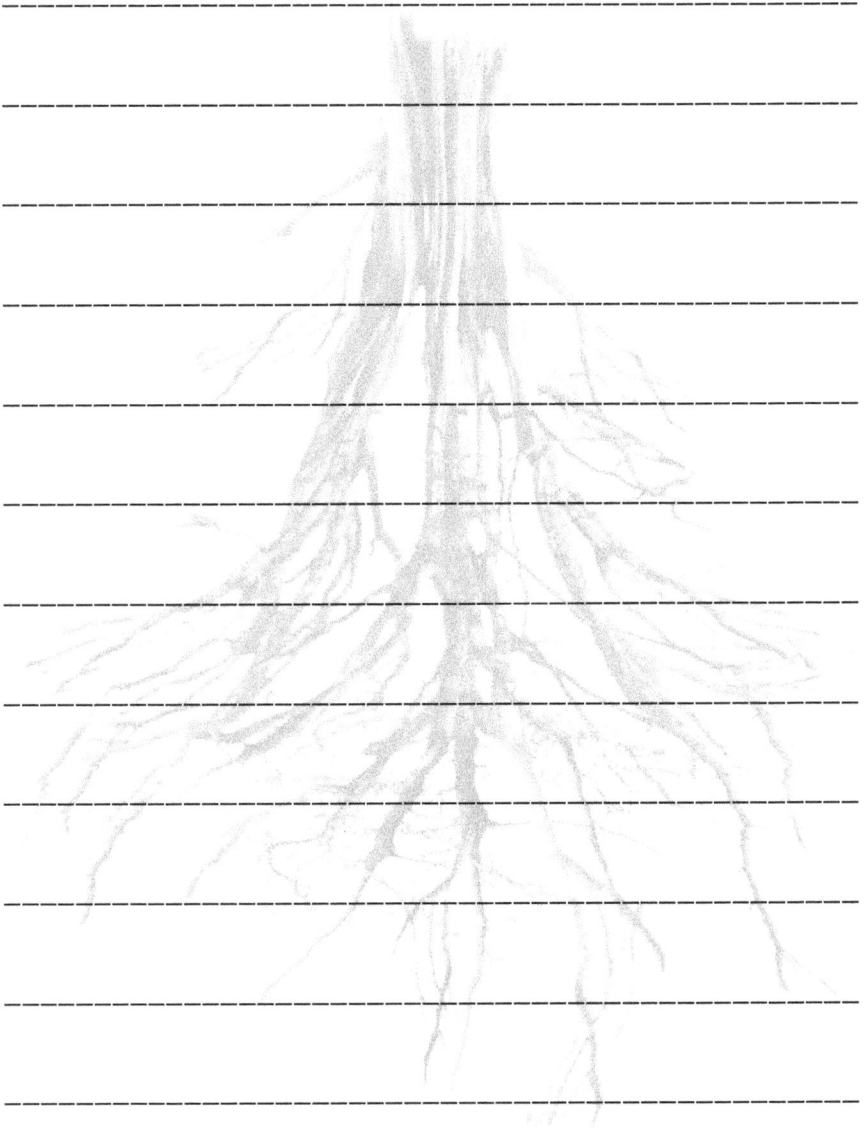

Chapter 4

Dead Ends

Have you ever traveled down a road that you were not sure about and then BOOM you come to a dead end? Oftentimes, voids lead to more voids, and before you know it, life seems to hit a dead end. I'm not sure what's worse though, realizing that the road can go no further or realizing that you have to try another way to get to your destination. The way your mind roams as well can be sickening. The never-ending questions that ask, "How can I get on the right path? Why was there not a sign stating the road was a dead end? Will I ever arrive at the place I'm trying to get to?" These are questions I asked myself whenever I was searching out my genetic background on my dad's side. I got a subscription to ancestry.com and went to work. I had to know! I wanted so desperately to find the answers. Who were my grandfather's parents? Where did he originate from? Where did he live? What was he like? Did he marry or have other children or was my daddy his only child? Could he sing or preach? QUESTIONS, QUESTIONS, QUESTIONS! Guess what? Every time I seemed to have a lead, I'd come to a screeching halt and a dead end. It was discouraging and heart wrenching. I'd search that website for hours, days, and weeks. Every turn led to nowhere. I was so frustrated. Most of all, it hurt. It hurt because I was searching to fill the void, but each time it was left wide open. Therefore, I eventually lost hope in the search.

Proverbs 13:12 states that Hope deferred makes the heart sick (KJV). A lot of people you encounter or have given the title "stuck" could be showing manifestation of a deferred heart. So many people underestimate the power of emotions in our lives. This is why the bible teaches us in 2 Corinthians 10:5 to cast down imaginations and every high thing that exalteth itself against the knowledge of God, and bringing into captivity every thought to the obedience of Christ (KJV). Actually, if you tell me the condition of a person's mind, I can tell you the manifested symptoms they carry. As a man thinketh in his heart, so is he (Proverbs 23:7)! I have one quick question for you. Did you notice the correlation between the heart and the mind? Naturally, you would think that the scripture would say "As a man thinketh with his BRAIN, but the scripture stated a person thinks with their heart. What a person feels in their heart influences their mind, actions, and behaviors whether it is verbalized or not. It's a heart issue. Let's go deeper if you will. If the behavior or broken mentality is the fruit, then where is the root? I'm glad you asked. The root that needs treating is in the heart. Notice I said treating instead of digging up. There are some things we experience in life that should not be irradicated nor eliminated. They should undergo

36

treatment in order to preserve them to a whole state again. I think it is wise to remember and recall some experiences from a healed standpoint. There is nothing like a good knowledgeable teacher who underwent a healing process. This is where the Christian world gathers and shares testimonies. That's the purpose of the trial in the first place; to be able to say, "Been there, done that, got the t-shirt" in some situations WITH SURVIVAL is a blessing! Every dead end does not have to be viewed as the end. It all depends on the way you look at it. I can hear you saying that coming to a dead end is HORRIBLE! I'd like to reply by saying, no, it may FEEL or LOOK horrible, but dead ends can be positively viewed as a turnaround point. There is always room for change in any situation. Here is one positive thing about a dead end. It's always room to backtrack and start again. Never think that a dead end is your destiny. That kind of thinking is where people adapt the mind of defeat. They feel defeated in their hearts and minds, therefore it spills over into their actions.

Let's look at what the spirit of defeat looks like in scripture. Let's walk to John 5: 1-15. I will pause for a second and let you get your bible out or at least google the scripture. I trust that you took a moment to read or familiarize yourself with the scenario in scripture. Well, let's dig into it. This lame fella had come to a dead end in life (as he felt). He had been so used to being down until getting up was not even on his mind. Thirty-eight years of being like this. He is stuck. Look at his surroundings. He was surrounded by people in disabled conditions and

37

in the same predicament as he. Well, let's dig further and eavesdrop on his conversation with Jesus. Jesus asks him a simple question of, "Will you be made whole?" His response is pitiful, and it gives a powerful revelation if you choose to see it. First of all, verse 7 begins with calling him impotent (powerless, helpless, unable to take action). He replies. "Sir, I have no man to put me into the pool when the water is stirred up, but while I am coming, another steps down before me." There is so much revelation in that one statement alone that will enlighten you and illuminate the man's heart and spiritual condition. Let's dig further. First you hear an excuse, but it's deeper than that. He is really saying, I have no hope, I have no one in my corner, I have no reason to try again because I already know the outcome therefore, I'm already defeated. He is saying that there is no need in trying. Can you hear in the spirit his condition? This man feels as if he is at a dead end.

If you feel like you have reached a dead end in relationships, jobs, or just life in general, I need to encourage you to TURN AROUND and get to walking again! Here are some classic roots/spirits that accompany the spirit of defeat (not all inclusive and varies).

The	Spirit	of	Defeat
DEPRESSION	APATHY	GUILT	DEFENSIVE
ANGER	EXCUSES	SPIRITUAL BLINDNESS	EXCESSIVE TIREDNESS
INSOMNIA	ANXIETY	STRESS HEADACHES	SADNESS
PARANOIA	OFFENCE	IRRITABLE	LAZINESS

Can I be transparent for a quick moment? Will you please slide me a "mercy pill" so that I can share this statement? Precious one, God sometimes allows you to become or feel defeated because that's when He can do His best work within us! I mean think about it, we are designed to need a champion in our corner, and if God allowed us to be strong and self-sufficient with every trial, then when would we ever admit that we need Him? If we never exhaust all of our efforts, how will we truly know that we have a miracle working God on our side? If we never have a need, why would we pray or communicate with our Father in Heaven? I've felt defeated more times than I care to admit, but I can honestly say that just because I felt defeated, it didn't mean that I was truly defeated. No, I simply cried out to God in the midst of my exhaustion, and the One who is NEVER DEFEATED came to my rescue. Hey, that's what a good father does. Let's pray so that He can come and rescue you too!

Father we cry out to you! You are our shield and great reward. You are the lifter of our heads. I pray for my friends that are reading this book right now. They are feeling the spirit of defeat in specific areas of their lives even now. Father, your people are going through. Someone is feeling depressed because they can't see a better future. Someone may feel like a failure simply because life has caused abrupt changes. Someone feels stuck because they have no strength to fight any longer. I pray that you show up as the Champion that I have found you to be. Breathe a fresh wind upon them now, a wind of change, a wind of strength, and a wind of direction. How can we boast about you unless you show up and show out for us? We will be so careful to give you ALL the glory because it belongs to you and you alone. In JESUS'S name we seal this prayer. Amen and Amen!

CHAPTER STUDY SECTION

Chapter 4: Dead End

A DEAD END CAN BE A MISERABLE EXPERIENCE. YOU ARE ON YOUR WAY SOMEWHERE, THEN IT ABRUPTLY STOPS. AS STATED IN THIS CHAPTER, LET'S EXAMINE THE MAN AT THE POOL A LITTLE FURTHER. WE'RE NOT TOLD HOW OLD HE IS, BUT THIRTY-EIGHT YEARS IS A LONG TIME TO DEPEND ON OTHERS! IN ADDITION, HIS SURROUNDINGS WERE BAD. THEY WERE BY A SHEEP MARKET! IT'S BAD ENOUGH TO BE STUCK, BUT TO BE IN A NOISY, STINKY ENVIRONMENT IS A WHOLE OTHER LEVEL OF MISERY. NOW THIS IS A DEAD END. WE NOW HAVE JESUS ENTERING THE SCENE, AND HE IS NOT CONCERNED ABOUT THE CIRCUMSTANCES BECAUSE HE IS A RULE BREAKER, SO HE DOESN'T NEED THE POOL. WHY WOULD JESUS NEED WHAT HE CREATED? HOWEVER, THIS MAN COULD NOT FATHOM BEING HEALED WITHOUT BEING PLACED IN THE POOL. MANY TIMES, WE CAN BECOME SO OVERWHELMED BY THE FACTS THAT WE FORGET TO ACTIVATE OUR FAITH. SOCIETY CAN SAY ONE THING ABOUT YOU, BUT JESUS CAN CHANGE YOUR SITUATION. ONCE THIS MAN REALIZED WHO WAS IN HIS PRESENCE, HIS DESIRE BECAME HIS REALITY. HE WAS ABLE TO DO SOMETHING HE HAD NEVER DONE BEFORE: RISE, TAKE UP HIS BED, AND WALK.

HAVE YOU REACHED A DEAD END? IF SO, HOW CAN YOU TURN AROUND?

41

Root Nourishment. WHEN OPERATING IN FAITH, YOU WILL BE ABLE TO DO THINGS THAT ONCE SEEMED IMPOSSIBLE. THERE IS STRENGTH IN JESUS FOR YOU TO GET UP AND WALK AGAIN.

Chapter Notes and Thoughts

_____

_____

_____

_____

_____

_____

_____

_____

_____

_____

Chapter 5

<u>Entanglements</u>

Whoooo-chhyyee! If there was a chapter that I could say that describes many in the world today, it would be this one!! I mean this is one that if you would be honest, you'd confirm that at some point or another you have experienced a serious entanglement. No, I'm not talking about the cute or simple stuff that only requires a simple, "let me make a quick decision to get out of this mess." I'm referring to the LORD IF YOU JUST HELP ME OUT... I PROMISE I WILL NEVER GET INTO THIS FOOLISHNESS AGAIN BECAUSE I SEE NO OTHER WAY OUT OF THIS MESS BUT YOU! It happens sometimes, and honestly, it's easy to become entangled in situations. It could be a job, marriage, friendship, church, organization, or a mixture of more than one. It could be a number of things. Nevertheless, if something or someone is draining the life out of you or hindering you from the next level, may I suggest you check for an entanglement?

What is an entanglement? It is defined as a compromising or complicated relationship or situation. In my words, I would describe it as being actively involved in something that seems impossible to be free without harm to self or other persons involved. A lot of times these types of relationships are formed due to seeking to fill voids in our lives. What does this look like in real life? I'm glad you asked! Okay let's visit ole Father Abraham in the scriptures. Y'all know him, right? Of course you do because we are heirs of his promise. Well, ole Pop Abie- Abe had some situations going on because: 1. God gave him a promise that he would have a son in his old age (pre-Viagra days). On top of that, 2. His wife was walking around with hard boiled eggs in her womb that were just as dusty and old as she was. Anyway, they became impatient, so Sarah offered her handmaid Hagar as a sidepiece for Pop Abey-Abe to sleep with. Man! Let's pause right there and understand that this is the first biblical episode of "Days of Our Lives" sidepiece drama edition! Okay, the sidepiece (Hagar) gets pregnant by Pop Abe, and she gives birth to his son. She named him Ishmael. Harmless right? I mean his WIFE was the one that suggested this solution anyway so no harm no foul, especially since there was verbal consent. NOT! This is a classic ENTANGLEMENT! How did it start? EMOTIONALLY! They did not want to wait on God, so they allowed their impatience, low self-esteem, immature reasoning, and poor views of their ability to lead them into this relationship entanglement. How could I say all of those adjectives to describe their emotional state? Easy. Emotions speak louder than your voice. I can tell where a person is in life simply by weighing their words against their actions. Your mouth can say, "God, I trust you," but your emotions would drive your actions to prove if you meant what you said. Let's pause for a minute and think about that truth. Do we really mean what we say? You can say that you know how to forgive, but what do your actions prove? You can proclaim that you are a woman of virtue, but what do your daily actions portray? You can boast by verbalizing that you are a grown man, but do you have grown men's principles? Do you gossip and tear down people when they are not present? Do you secretly envy in your heart while pressing the love button under folk's pictures on Facebook? When you say congratulations, do you really mean it, or are your mouth and fingers functioning off of muscle memory? That's really something to think about. You can see Abraham's, Sarah's, and Hagar's emotions running rampant in the text of Genesis Chapter 16. I paraphrased the account, so please go back and read it in its original language, but we can see the fruit (their actions/reactions) based on the roots (the driving emotions of their hearts). No seriously, Abraham must feel less of a man because as each day and year pass, he is getting older but not producing the promise like God said, so he was desperate to prove his manhood and eager to go back to sowing his aging seeds with this young tender-roni if you know what I mean. Sarah was feeling less of a woman because she couldn't conceive, so in her low self-esteem and internal comparison, she offered Hagar. Hagar had no choice but to obey because she was a slave to Sarah. She had this false sense of importance because her baby-daddy was Abraham! She could give him something his wife couldn't. She was feeling all pumped and precious, but in actuality she was nothing more than a servant in its simplest form. Wow! Do you see how easily that situation turned into a complicated entanglement? Oh, it gets better! Hagar birthed her son, and sure enough Sarah becomes jealous! The Lord spoke to Abraham and Sarah again and said in a nutshell, "I know you think you have fixed this up as my promise, but I said SARAH would bear a son and through HIM would the promise come!" A few years passed and Sarah, sure enough, gets pregnant and gives birth to Isaac. Well, the brothers (Isaac and Ishmael) grow up together and one day Sarah looks out from the tent and sees Ishmael picking with Isaac! OH HECK NAW! All Hell broke loose, and Sarah goes and tells Abraham, "Look, ya little baby momma and her knocked kneed slew footed son gots to go! They don't have to leave Canaan, but she got to get up out of my tent (Lady Shae's translation)!" Well, of course Abraham loves his son Ishmael, but Sarah is his wife and you know the saying, "Happy Wife-Happy Life." Momma bear was not happy (it's her own fault though). Guess what Pop Abe does? You guessed it. He told Hagar to pack up and leave and take little Ish with her! The only child support he gave to his first baby momma was ONE BOTTLE OF WATER! LAWD HAVE MERCY! Look at Hagar! She has to be feeling used, abused, and manipulated, as well as embarrassed for being brought into a situation that had nothing to do with her originally. She does what she is told (leave the premises), and now she is out to fend for herself as well as her young child! This is horrible! Yet, God loves all parties enough to intervene and help them all. I have no judgment for Abraham, Sarah, Hagar, nor their children. You know why? I have no judgement because life happens. One emotion can send you on a downhill spiral, and before you know it, you have gotten entangled in any and everything along the way!

Ok let's talk friend. Come and sit by me for a minute. What has entangled you over the years or better yet lately? I come to suggest with all sincerity of heart to say Sis/Bro IT'S TIME! Time for what? It's time for you to get free from the things that have you bound and entangled. Aren't you tired of the same old things trapping you up? Oh ok, are we going to pretend like you have nothing there? Well, let me go ahead and say that you have something even if it's a self-sabotaging way of thinking. Here is the dilemma that traps many people of the Christian faith. We have preconceived notions of how entanglements should look embedded into our minds already. I will say that every entanglement does not have to involve sin, but all of us deal with weights. What is a weight? A weight is something that tends to slow us down! Hebrews 12:1 says, "Wherefore seeing we also are compassed about with so great a cloud of witnesses, let us lay aside every weight, and the sin which doth so easily beset us, and let us run with patience the race that is set before us (KJV). There are all kinds of entanglements, and some have nothing to do with adultery, lying, stealing, or cheating. Those are obvious things, but what about judging others without cause, prejudice, jealousy, slothfulness,

47

pride, and poor money management? Do you lose sleep or worry over things you have no control over? Does something as simple as a person breathing hard tick you off? Good Lord, (insert eye roll) what if the person has asthma or something! Here is a big one, ROAD RAGE! How many people have you cursed out in your mind simply because they slowed you down ten seconds or so? Have you considered that un-forgiveness runs rampant among church folks? What about holding grudges or making pledges and vows to never do things simply because they put us in our feelings? What about being competitive in your heart and never becoming content with what you have? Are you too prideful to admit that you need help? Are you above seeking counseling for deep rooted issues? All I know is this, entanglements are no fun, and they are Satan's belts that tie us down from reaching our destiny. I'm not sure how much time we have left before Christ returns for His second coming, but I'm confident enough to declare that we have no more time to waste being entangled! I desired to be free, and I know you do too. Let's pray about it together!

Father, we come to you seeking help. We need help to search the complicated areas of our lives. We ask that you shine a light on unholy alliances and bonds we've created over the years. Any habits Dear Father that we have fallen into we ask that you give us power to destroy the bands and spirit of constrictions in the Name of Jesus. Father we desire to be free and whom your son sets free is free indeed! We commit these areas of our lives unto you now in Jesus's name Amen!

CHAPTER STUDY SECTION

Chapter 5: Entanglements

IT SEEMS AS IF THE WORD "ENTANGLEMENT" HAS JUST NOW REACHED POPULARITY, BUT ENTANGLEMENTS HAVE BEEN TRAPPING PEOPLE FOR YEARS. THESE TYPES OF TRAPS HAPPEN WHEN WE OBEY OUR FLESH INSTEAD OF BEING LED BY THE SPIRIT OF GOD. ABRAHAM AND SARAH WERE PROMISED A CHILD WHEN THEY WERE SEVENTY-FIVE AND SIXTY-FIVE YEARS OLD, RESPECTIVELY. HOWEVER, IMPATIENCE WAS THEIR MAIN DOWNFALL. SOMETIMES OUR SILENT SEASONS AND NOT SEEING THE HAND OF GOD LIKE WE DESIRE ARE BECAUSE WE'VE BECOME ENTANGLED WITH SOMETHING UNGODLY. GOD WILL NOT CONTEND WITH THE DESIRES OF THE FLESH; THEREFORE, HE TELLS US TO CHOOSE WHOM WE WILL SERVE. OUR CHOICES ARE POWERFUL, AND EVEN THOUGH ENTANGLEMENTS CAN BE COMPLICATED, RISKY, EMBARRASSING AND MANY OTHER NEGATIVE THINGS, AT THE END OF THE DAY WE HAVE A CHOICE TO MAKE. WE CAN ASK GOD TO FREE US, OR WE CAN STAY BOUND. EITHER WAY IT'S YOUR CHOICE, BUT FREEDOM IS MUCH BETTER THAN BEING BOUND.

How often do you find yourself caught up in the middle of things that had absolutely nothing to do with you?

Do you find yourself getting involved or volunteering your help for things you really don't have time for?

Root Nourishment: Never tie yourself to things and people that you were never designed to be tied to. Your freedom depends upon it.

Chapter Notes and Thoughts

Chapter 6

The Cave Experience

Have you ever wanted to run away? No, seriously, like skip several towns and just hit the reset button and act like certain parts of your life were never experienced or existed? Believe it or not, more people feel that way more often than you think. Most times it is a temporary and fleeting thought, but for some people it is a real heart's desire.

Cave experiences are not necessarily a bad thing. Honestly, we have a built-in human response for whenever we face unfavorable odds. It's natural to want to withdraw and retreat for different reasons. Spiritual Caves are meant to be therapeutic in a safe way. Here is where I have learned to draw the line of deciding if the withdrawal is therapeutic or detrimental. It can be summed up into one question and that is, "Why did you retrieve in the first place?" In other words, what was your reason for feeling the need to hide? What is the root of the issue? It's one thing to enter a cave to recoup or to heal a wounded heart, but it's never ok to enter one with the intention of laying down to die!

Now, can we step away from the spiritual side of things for a second and look at it in a natural sense? I don't profess to be a psychologist, yet if you serve people on a daily basis, you can't deny that you can have the same set of circumstances across the board, but everyone will approach and respond to those circumstances differently. I personally think this is an area where Christians have to mature daily in their thinking in general and could lend more grace to others. I said all of that to say this- WE ALL GET PHYSICALLY TIRED at some point or another. Sometimes the things that wear us down are our emotions, thought processes, and spiritual condition that drives us to that exhaustion point. Secondly, it is natural to want to rest! That's actually our internal body alarm system letting us know, "Hey, you are doing too much! Take it easy for a few days!" The thing that is not natural is the desire to faint or die even though many people have pondered both notions at some point in their lives. The cares of the world will drain the Jesus out of you literally if you allow it. Whenever you come across a person of such, please handle them with care. Let's go a few steps further in the natural. I often say this phrase; if you understand the nature of a thing, its action will never surprise you. If you encounter a thief and you fail to hide your valuables in their presence, then YOU are the one who needs the reality check. The reality is that a thief will steal, and you have to act according to their habit. Well, if a person is emotionally disabled then why do we expect them to do amazing things that require emotional stability? It's not possible, especially if you need consistency. This is where we become disappointed with certain relationship experiences. We sometimes hand things of great value such as our hearts and dreams to people who are not emotionally capable of holding the weight. My youngest child and daughter is almost thirteen years old. She's a quick learner and multi-talented. That girl can literally do just about anything, but her thought process is fleeting. She cares more about meeting up with her friends in a virtual video game regardless of the fact that she has the capability and gifting of a grown person. She could very well make money doing some of the things she is naturally gifted at. Now bear with me, I'm going somewhere. She has worked alongside me helping with video productions and graphics and I pay her. Now, would I be smart to weigh her down with several assignments and think she will have them completed by a certain important deadline? No! That would not be wise nor smart at all. Why? As stated before, she has the attention span and mind of a typical 12/13-year-old. I also forestated, her mind is fleeting which is natural for her age group. I find myself frustrated because she can't see what I can see, but in actuality she is not mature enough to fully understand her giftings and future yet. Therefore, I treat her accordingly. The right amount of negative pressure from me could cause the wrong reaction. Do you see where I'm going with this? Well, it's the same way when it relates to emotionally traumatized or emotionally disabled people. We set ourselves up for failure in so many areas whenever we lay things at their feet that are too heavy for them. That's why it's important to be healed, delivered, and set free! What if you are one healing away from receiving the strength you need to rise to your next opportunity? Just like many of us are great parents and understand what our children can handle is the same way God our heavenly father knows how much we can bear. He will not lay major responsibilities on a broken spirit. Therefore, you have to chase the root cause of the experiences. You have to go back to the place where it all fell apart. You have to face the harsh truths once again even if it's nothing but getting closure. Many run into caves to die, but that will not happen on my watch. Can you hear me searching for you? God is sending me after you. and I'm singing in my calmest voice saying," Come out, come out, wherever you are!" It's time my sisters and brothers. The world needs you and your testimonies, but you can't share them from within a cave. Your truths can set others free. I'm not able to write this because I'm so smart and intellectual. I'm able to describe these dark moments because I've retrieved into caves far more times than I care to admit. If I can be more candid and truthful, a few times I even entered with the hopes of laying down to die. Thanks be unto God who always sent someone after me to minister to my dying soul. Here are a few roots that I had to go and dig up, and if I may have a transparent grace, I will share them with you. Here are ten things I found out about me upon post cave evaluations.

1. I bore false burdens.

2. I was an extreme people pleaser.

3. I gave myself more importance in the life of some people than I should have.

4. I was insecure.

5. I was easily offended unjustly.

6. I am an over-thinker (I still deal with this).

7. I harbored guilt in my heart.

8. I was prone to spiritual abortion.

9. I tend to procrastinate.

10. I lived in fear.

I just shared ten roots that I've dug up over the years, and I pray that you can find out exactly what causes you to retrieve or shut down in certain areas of your lives. Here is a MAJOR root that holds and entangles all of the other ones tightly and binds them together. It is the root of pride. I pray that the spirit of pride is dismantled from your life even as you consider the things and people that hold you hostage in your heart. Pride can hinder you from your next level in God. Pull up the roots so that the ground you stand on will become freer! There is a light shining outside of your cave. Walk towards it! There is something that God wants you to see.

Let's go to God in prayer about it.

Father God in the matchless name of Jesus. We ask you to come and get us where we are. Many reading this are hiding in caves from the mere pressures of life. Lord, someone even entered without telling anyone they have retrieved in their heart. They smile on the outside, but they are severely wounded on the inside. Mend their broken places even as we speak. I pray that you send angels to minister to them and give them strength even now. Let them know that not only are you God on the mountaintops and in the valleys, but you are also God in the darkest corridors of spiritual caves. We thank you for the peace to know that healing belongs to us through Christ Jesus and victory is already ours. In Jesus's name I pray. Amen.

CHAPTER STUDY SECTION

Chapter 6: The Cave Experience

THE CAVE- A DARK PLACE, UNCERTAINTY, AND FEAR! THESE ARE JUST SOME OF THE EMOTIONS KING DAVID EXPERIENCED IN THE CAVE. HE WAS ANOINTED TO BE KING, BUT HIS PREDECESSOR (KING SAUL) WAS TRYING TO KILL HIM. HE ENDS UP RUNNING FOR HIS LIFE AND RETREATING IN A CAVE. LOOK AT HIS ANOINTING! HE IS ANOINTED TO BE KING BUT HIDING DUE TO HIS FEELINGS. I COME TO LET YOU KNOW THAT THE CAVE IS NOT A RESPECTER OF PERSONS. IT WILL HOUSE THE SAINT AS WELL AS A SINNER. IT DOESN'T MATTER WHO YOU ARE. IF YOU DESIRE TO WALK INTO ITS DARKNESS, IT WILL SURELY MEET YOU THERE. CAVES ARE NO FUN! ARE YOU HIDING IN ONE RIGHT NOW?

WHAT NEGATIVE EXPERIENCES HAVE LED YOU TO A CAVE EITHER NOW OR IN THE PAST?

DO YOU ALLOW PEOPLE OR WORLDLY SITUATIONS TO DEPRESS YOU?

DO YOU FIND YOURSELF TENDING TO OTHERS WHILE YOU SUFFER AND NEED HELP FOR YOURSELF?

Root Nourishment: SATAN WANTS YOU TO THINK THAT YOUR CAVE EXPERIENCE IS THE END, BUT THAT IS NOT GOD'S PLAN FOR YOU. SHAKE OFF ALL DOUBT AND DISCOURAGEMENT BY SPEAKING AND STANDING ON THE WORD (JOSHUA 1:8).

Chapter Notes and Thoughts

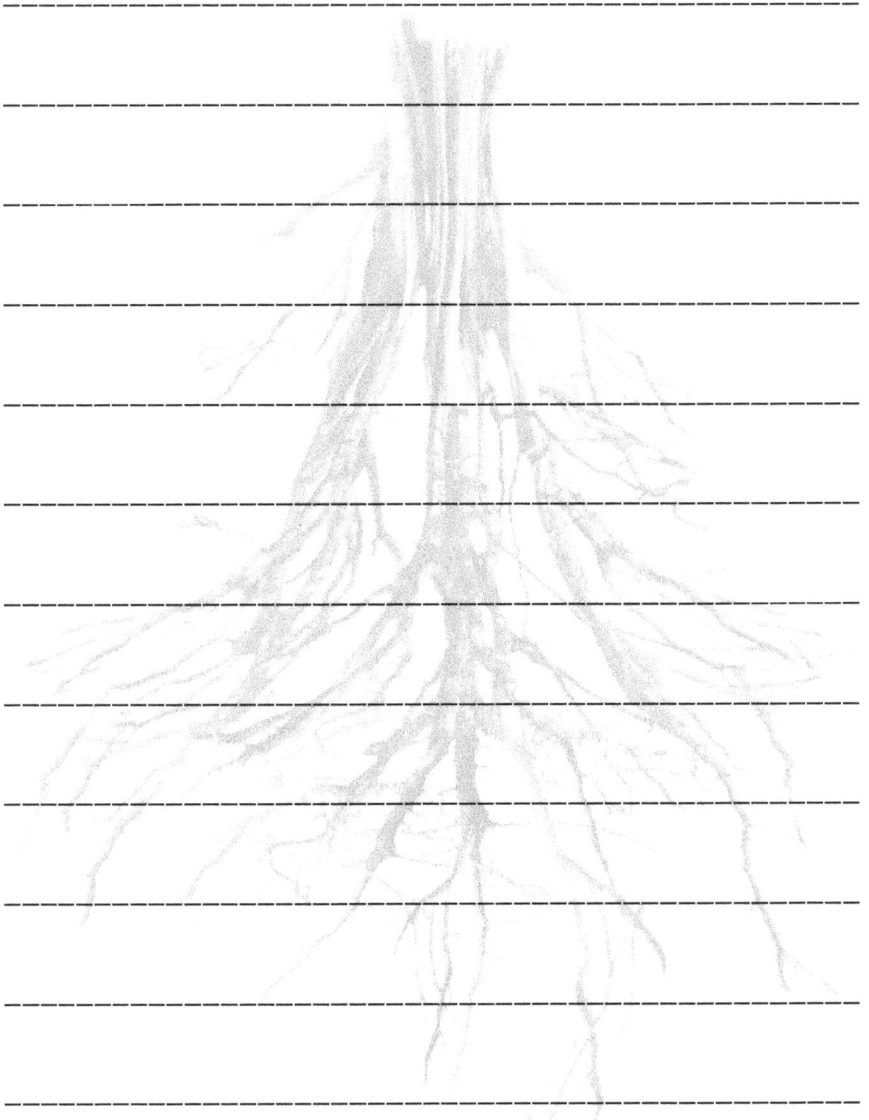

Chapter 7

<u>Seeing the Light</u>

Sometimes seeing hurts. Have you ever had an eye exam and the optometrist dilated your eyes to check behind the retina for health? Well, if you've had that procedure done before, then you know that upon exiting the office the staff will hand you a dark pair of shades. The shades are necessary because sudden exposure to light causes blurred vision and pain. For another example, have you ever been in a dark theater or room for hours at a time, and when it's time to exit you step outside in the sun? The natural response is to cover your eyes to allow them time to adjust to the light exposure. Well, spiritually you have to be careful whenever you emerge from a dark cave into the light. What you see and become exposed to may cause pain and can be spiritually blinding temporarily. This is not a bad thing, and it is quite natural to experience it, but if you are not prepared and forewarned it could cause you more damage and harm than good.

Truth serves as light in our lives, and sometimes the truth hurts. With that being said, never downplay the miracle of being able to see the truth. Please make note: The pain is temporary, but having vision is transforming. I tell people this statement often, "I'd rather see and hurt than to be blind and comfortable." Read that again. Did you get what I said? Look, here is the sad reality of the world we now live in. Many people choose comfort over truth and think nothing of it. There are literally people in our midst that will get fighting mad over a truth versus losing their comfort. This is not shocking. The bible speaks of this in the last days. So many things are being accepted nowadays. Right is now being called wrong and wrong is now labeled as right! My goodness! What price are you willing to pay to remain comfortable? Why are so many sacrificing their vision for the sake of familiarity? This is a crucial hour in the world, but I want to keep my vision at all costs! Honestly, I once was blind (spiritually), but now I see. I like seeing better than being blind.

I've had to face many truths. One that stung the most during my genetic search was realizing that there is simply not enough information available to piece my fraternal history together. Y'all, that hurts. After hours and hours of searching census records and genealogy websites, I'd always come to a dead end. Today I'm okay with that truth. I've come to the realization that whatever God allowed to know was best for me. It was not predestined in His will for me to know the specifics. I am not saying that it doesn't cross my mind from time to time, but I'm saying it no longer blinds me. The light of the truth of "It's just not meant for me to know'' allows me to see well. I didn't get to this peace overnight though. I went through several emotional stages along the way. I experienced many hiccups and turns while traveling along the search path. One of the greatest lessons I have learned is that it's so easy to focus on a set outcome until the income (wealth of valuable lessons obtained through experiences) goes unnoticed. What truths have shed light on your darkest days that led you to hurt but see?

Many things hinder our sight during post cave moments. Your heart and emotions are very fragile, and you have to make sure you pray about those who attach to you when you are gaining strength after a dark storm that left you vulnerable. Believe me or not, there are people who wait patiently for your vulnerable moments so that they can gain the opportunity to slither into your life. I don't want to promote fear and distrust. I simply want you to be cautious because what you see and the truths surrounding you can be shocking yet freeing. Nevertheless, seeing the light is a good thing.

What are some things that hinder our sight? I'm glad you asked. I will name a few, and they are: a rebellious heart, depression, a broken spirit, confusion, esteem problems, ungodly connections, disobedience, rejection and offense, bitterness, pride, denial, and witchcraft. This is not an all-inclusive list, but what I named just barely scratches the surface. Anything that keeps you blind or anything or anyone who benefits from your lack of vision can be dangerous to your growth and progress. Do you know that some people love the fact that you just can't "see the truth?" They love it because they benefit from your lack of vision. They hope that you never come to the realization of how powerful you really are, and the day that your eyes open is the day that you no longer need to depend on or be used by them. That's why it's so crucial for you to gain your sight to see the light. What is it that God wants to reveal to you through the light of His truths concerning you? Are you ready for this? Well, the primary thing that God wants you to realize is that HE WAS WITH YOU THE ENTIRE TIME. There is not one moment of your life where you walked alone. Notice I didn't say you didn't feel alone because that could be possible. Yet, the truth is that HE never left you alone. Think about it. You were in some major storms but who do you think it was that delivered you? Who do you think kept you from losing your mind? Who do you think protected you during your crazy stages? Who kept you safe when you were around dangers unaware? Who do you think it was that told you not to commit suicide when you thought your life was not worth living? Who do you think it was that filled that hole in your heart when those who swore they loved you walked away without a second thought? Oh, it was GOD BABY! Nobody but God and he NEVER left your side! That is the first thing you need to understand! The second thing God wants you to see is that you are much stronger and powerful than you realize. Many people would have crumbled under the set circumstances you were functioning under. You survived, and that is commendable and noteworthy. Thirdly, (this will stretch you a little, but I will say it just the same) YOUR story should be told. Do you understand that someone surrounding you right now could benefit and be encouraged by the things you have endured? Never downplay the miracles in your life. Never be embarrassed of your journey. Nothing was done in vain. You survived for a reason and that reason was for you to point someone else to the light.

Growing up I never viewed myself as an author. I never imagined that I'd share my thoughts, defeats, and victories with many people around the world. I never considered that people would find healing through my pain yet, here I am. I made a conscious decision to share. You should consider sharing too.

Let's pray about it! Father in the Name of Jesus. Thank you for shining the light on us! Thank you for finding us when we were hiding in darkness and calling us into your marvelous light. Father, we understand that sometimes we get sidetracked and distracted and we lose sight. Please shine your light on us so that we can see. Open our eyes and command that the blinders fall off concerning any areas that have us blind. Mainly, open the eyes of our hearts because we want to see you. We thank you and trust you with every dark place in our lives. In Jesus's mighty name. Amen

Chapter Study Section

Chapter 7: Seeing the Light

Zacchaeus is a good example of seeing the light. He was a low-down tax collector who became rich from beating people out of their money. I'm not sure what all Zacchaeus heard about Jesus but one thing for sure, he needed to "see" what he was all about. When he heard that Jesus was passing through Jericho, he desperately wanted to get in Jesus's presence, but he was too short in statue and the crowd was too large. He wanted to see more than he desired to be comfortable, so he ran ahead of the crowd and climbed a sycamore tree. He was sick of living in the dark, so he climbed high to see the light! Salvation and deliverance were what he found upon the end of his search.

How bad do you want to see?

How do you react to truths when revealed?

Do you tend to live in denial about obvious situations?

Root Nourishment: No one can judge you for being in the dark unknowingly. It happens sometimes but whenever truth is available it is beneficial to move towards the light so that you can at least have the proper sight to safely proceed to the nest.

Chapter Notes and Thoughts

Chapter 8

The End of the Search

There is an old song that I love to hear. Even as a child, whenever I'd hear the lyrics, an overwhelming sense of unexplainable peace would enter my soul. The lyrics simply state:

Farther along we'll know all about it,

Farther along we'll understand why

 Cheer up my brother, live in the sunshine,

We'll understand it... All by and by!

Now that I'm older, I truly grasp why those lyrics gave me peace. There have been many instances where I've endured and weathered various storms. I had no clue as to why I was going through so much only to see weeks, months, or years later down the road the real purpose. Have you ever endured painful times to later understand the "whys" and revelation of their purpose? Yep, it happens like that sometimes. Now, I'm about to throw a curve ball so make sure you catch this next statement. There are some things you may encounter, and you may never understand what they were all about. Well shucks! It happens like that as well. However, I feel that a degree of wisdom and strength accompanies those moments.

I can't say that I understand the lack of my Father's lineage information, but I will honestly say that I no longer search (purposely). I realized that in the mid to late 1800s, African Americans were considered as property and not humans. They came from various places and were stripped of their original identity. They were given the last names of their slave owners. They were not even counted on the census unless their slave owners listed them. It is just so many underlying causes that make the search hard. Do I believe that my grandfather had other siblings? Absolutely! I can look at other families whom we share the same last name with, and I see my resemblance in some of their faces. I see my dad's smile and expressions in some of their faces as well. We share similar personalities and talents. The spiritual root of singing and preaching is very strong among the Reel family far and near. The joking and wittiness are undeniable. Most of all, the root of family oneness is unmatched. I can spot a real Reel any day of the week. I can't pin the exact location where our (my siblings and I) branch sprouts from the Reel family tree, but I know that we belong. I had to come to the resting conclusion that it was just not predestined for us to know the specifics. Here is one wisdom key that I own now, and it changed my entire perspective when it comes down to understanding why I went through all of these changes and experiences over their years. God was trying to teach me something. I now realize that God was not interested in revealing to me the specifics about my fraternal heritage, but he was adamant on teaching me about my ETERNAL HERITAGE. I will go ahead and admit that IF my daddy would have been allowed to live and be in my life this whole time, I would probably be the most entitled, spoiled, narcissistic, person you'd ever met. Like seriously, I can see that was the road that I was headed down, but that was not God's plan for my life. He planned for me to go on this search to get to the realization that my REAL ROOTS are grounded in HIM. I will not lie; I sorely miss my earthly daddy, but that's the human side that feels that way. I can also vouch that God has been EVERY BIT of what He promised in Psalms 27:10! That man (God) has been everything for me and more. He has been an amazing Heavenly Father. I've received mercy and grace at His hand. He's given me gifts, talents and earthly possessions. He's led me all the way up to this present moment, and He will continue to lead me in the future. He has protected me from dangers seen and unseen. He has chastised me when needed and rewarded me when deserved. He loves me unconditionally, and He ALWAYS listens to my plea. He says no to some things I ask for, and He sometimes makes me wait for the things I may not be ready to receive just yet. Either way, I can honestly say that God has been the perfect Father for me! With that being said, I have not always liked everything that He allowed to come my way. It doesn't feel good to be told no, wait, or grow up, but what child loves everything their parent does? I've gained peace in knowing that I have a full identity and a prosperous future in Christ. I trust Him with the details of my life and the concerns of my heart. It was only in Him that I found closure, and I stopped my physical search of carnal things I can't trace. The only things that I search and chase to correct are errors in my life that lead to non-productivity. I had to learn that all roots were not planted by God, and the things that Satan planted when revealed have to be removed. I refuse to pass down toxic traits to my children. It all stops with me. I fully understand that the search was never about my earthly father, but it was to lead me closer to my Heavenly Father! Guess what else I understood? When I grasped that God was leading me to Him, I then found my earthly father and his lineage! They are all resting with God, and one day I will get a chance to see everyone I once searched for! All roads led to God, and with Him were my answers and ancestors.

I pray that this short book helped you in some way or another. It was surely therapeutic for me while writing this. I pray that by now you understand that you don't have to search any further. God, our Father, has all of the answers with Him! Go and ask Him what you need to know. The scripture states that if any man lacks wisdom, let him ask of God who giveth to all men liberally (James 1:5). Over the years, I've needed wisdom to do many things, and it was mainly things that no one else had time to teach or show me. I didn't give up. I asked God, and my Daddy taught me how to win! My Daddy is a winner, and the seed of winning is within me! I will let you in on a little secret, but don't tell anyone that I told you! If Jesus is your Lord and Savior, then we have the same Daddy! Winning is your portion as well my sister and brother. What are you waiting for? The search is over! Get up and get to succeeding! We've struck gold with this root! The root of Jesse (Isaiah 11:11) runs through us! WE ARE NOTHING TO PLAY WITH! Strength is our name, and WE WIN!

Let's thank God in prayer for His infinite wisdom! Father God, we thank you for being everything we need and more! We thank you for every moment in life that you allowed us to go through. We thank you for your protection and we thank you even more for your loving kindness. Father, help those who took this journey with me to experience the peace that you've given! Help them to understand that some things will be revealed only at the end of time. You are our Alpha and Omega, our Beginning and End, you are the First and Last and most of all you are our Father and Friend. Comfort your people now and help calm their hearts and minds. Let them rest knowing that you have predestined our lives, and nothing is out from under your rule and jurisdictions. You have the whole world in your hands. We give you praise, honor and glory! We seal this prayer in Jesus's name, Amen

CHAPTER STUDY SECTION

Chapter 8: The End of the Search

IN THE BOOK OF JOB, YOU WILL FIND HIS LIFE WAS PRETTY WELL OFF IN THE BEGINNING. HE WAS RICH AND HAD A BEAUTIFUL FAMILY. WHAT'S MOST NOTABLE ABOUT JOB IS THAT THE BIBLE PROCLAIMED THAT HE WAS A "PERFECT AND UPRIGHT" MAN. JOB LOVED HIS GOD. WELL, IF YOU KNOW THE STORY YOU KNOW THAT HE ENDED UP GOING THROUGH VARIOUS TRIALS AND TESTS AT THE HAND OF GOD AND SATAN. GOD ALLOWED SATAN TO SEND HARDSHIP JOB'S WAY IN ORDER FOR HIM TO TURN HIS HEART AWAY FROM GOD. JOB SEARCHED MANY DAYS FOR ANSWERS AS TO WHAT HAD HE DONE WRONG FOR HIM TO EXPERIENCE SUCH HARDSHIP IN LIFE. NOT ONLY THAT, JOB HAD THREE FRIENDS THAT CAME TO VISIT WITH HIM AND WEIGH IN ON HIS TROUBLE. JOB FOUND PEACE, AND CLARITY AT THE END OF HIS SEARCH. HE WAS RESTORED DOUBLE AFTER IT WAS ALL OVER. WHAT HAVE YOU FOUND OUT ABOUT YOUR LIFE IN HINDSIGHT OF SOME OF YOUR ROUGHEST TRIALS AND TESTS?

DO YOU SOMETIMES WONDER WHY YOU HAD TO GO THROUGH AND EXPERIENCE CERTAIN THINGS IN YOUR LIFE?

ARE YOU STILL SEARCHING FOR ANSWERS?

Root Nourishment: JOB PENNED A STATEMENT THAT CAN LEAD TO PEACE IF YOU ACCEPT HIS WISDOM. HE STATES IN JOB 13:15, "THOUGH HE SLAY ME, YET WILL I TRUST IN HIM." WE MAY NOT EVER UNDERSTAND EVERY ASPECT OF OUR LIVES, BUT WE CAN SURE DECIDE TO TRUST GOD WITH EVERY ASPECT OF OUR LIVES!

Chapter Notes and Thoughts

Random Roots

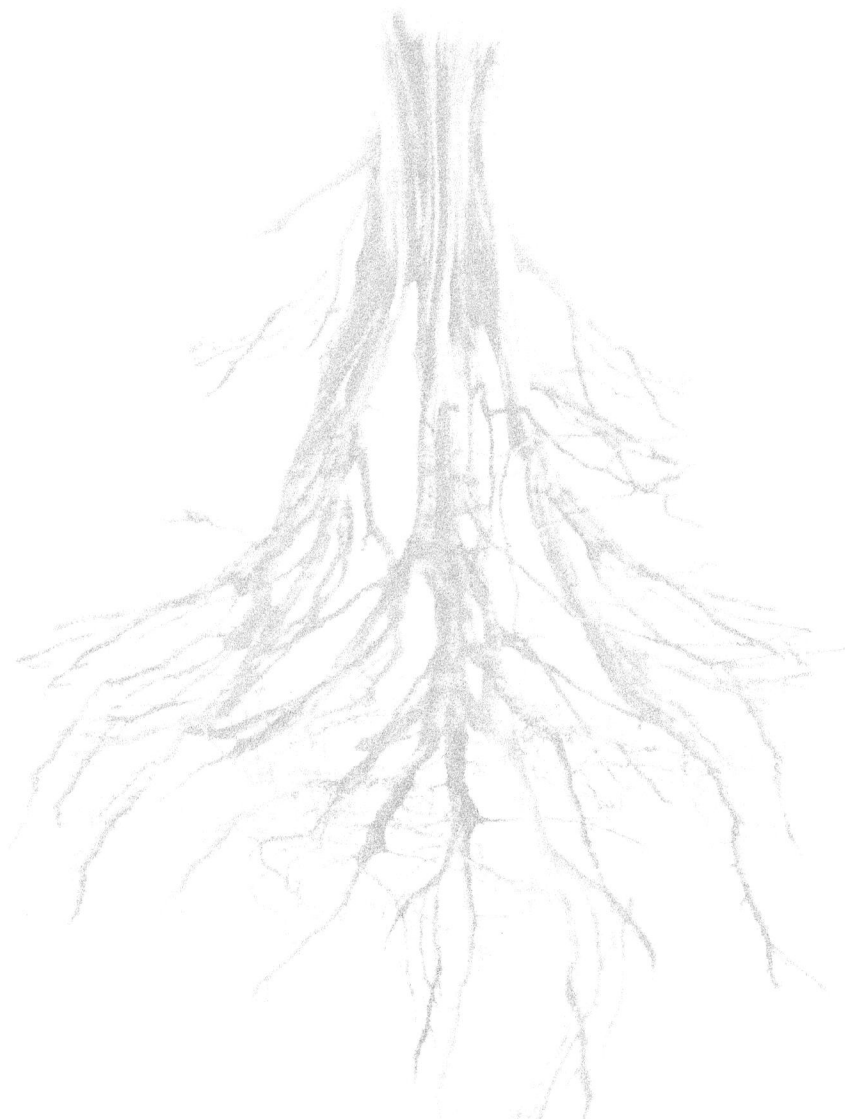

GENERATIONAL ROOTS

CREATE A FAMILY TRIVIA GAME OR FAMILY TREE WITH YOUR CHILDREN AND/OR GRANDCHILDREN AND ASK THEM TO "NAME THAT RELATIVE." THIS WILL PROMOTE AWARENESS OF FAMILY MEMBERS AND TEACH THEM THEIR FAMILY HERITAGE. BRING OUT ANY AMAZING STORIES, PICTURES, AND EVENTS THAT HAVE HAPPENED IN YOUR FAMILY! NOTE ANY FAMOUS RELATIVES OR MAJOR ACCOMPLISHMENTS. WHO ARE THE BEST COOKS IN THE FAMILY? ARE THERE ANY PROFESSIONALS IN YOUR FAMILY? WHO WAS THE FIRST TO GRADUATE COLLEGE? WHAT ARE THE FAMILY STRENGTHS AND ALSO WEAKNESSES? YOU CAN ONLY CORRECT WHAT YOU ARE WILLING TO CONFRONT. THIS ACTIVITY SHOULD ENLIGHTEN AND CREATE A STRONG FAMILY HISTORY AND BOND. MAKE SURE YOU UNDERSTAND THAT SOMETIMES LOOKING AT THE POSITIVE ACTIONS OF YOUR PAST RELATIVES CAN GIVE CLUES TO HIDDEN GIFTS AND TALENTS WITHIN YOURSELF. MY FAMILY IS FULL ON BOTH SIDES WITH CREATIVE AND INNOVATIVE GENES. I FOUND THE STRENGTH TO TRY SIMPLY BECAUSE OF THE PATHS THEY PAVED. THERE IS SOMETHING UNIQUE ABOUT EVERY FAMILY. FIND OUT WHAT IS SPECIAL ABOUT YOURS AND WORK THE GIFTS. LEGACY IS MEANT TO LIVE AND NOT DIE!

Notes and Thoughts

FAMILY ROOTS

ONE VIVID MEMORY I HAVE OF MY FATHER IS FROM THE FALL OF 1983. DADDY WAS PLOWING IN THE FIELD ACROSS THE ROAD, AND I WAS STANDING ON THE PORCH WATCHING HIM GO UP AND DOWN MAKING THE ROWS AS NEAT AS POSSIBLE. ALL OF A SUDDEN MOMMA RAN TO THE PORCH SCREEN DOOR AND SAID, "LORD, DAVE HAS FALLEN BEHIND THE PLOW." SHE GAVE A SLIGHT CHUCKLE BUT QUICKLY HOLLERED OUT TO HIM AND SAID, "HOLD THAT PLOW DAVE AND DON'T LET IT GO!" I DIDN'T UNDERSTAND WHY SHE WAS MORE FOCUSED ON HIM HOLDING THE PLOW RATHER THAN TELLING HIM TO GET UP! NOW THAT I'M OLDER AND HAVE A FAMILY OF MY OWN, I TOTALLY UNDERSTAND WHY IT WAS IMPORTANT FOR HIM TO HOLD ON TO THE PLOW. YOU SEE, DADDY HAD WORKED HARD ALL DAY, AND HE HAD ONLY A FEW MORE ROWS TO GO. HE HAD ALMOST FINISHED THE ENTIRE FIELD, AND IF HE WOULD HAVE LET GO OF THE PLOW IT WOULD HAVE GONE WILD AND DUG UP ALL OF THE PREVIOUS SEEDS HE HAD NEATLY PLANTED. NEEDLESS TO SAY, DADDY HELD ON TIGHT AND GOT BACK UP TO FINISH THE FIELD BECAUSE HE NEEDED THAT HARVEST TO COME THROUGH. THAT FOLLOWING SPRING HE TRANSITIONED TO HEAVEN ON APRIL 14, 1984. DUE TO HIM HOLDING THAT PLOW, WE (HIS FAMILY) ATE A LONG TIME BECAUSE HIS FALL HARVEST WAS PLENTIFUL. HE WAS IN HEAVEN, BUT HIS SEEDS FED US HERE ON EARTH! DO YOU KNOW AND UNDERSTAND THAT OUR SPIRITUAL JOURNEY IS SIMILAR TO MY

DEAR CHILDHOOD MEMORY? OUR CHRISTIAN JOURNEY IS THE FIELD, OUR CHARACTER IS THE PLOW, AND OUR INFLUENCE ARE THE SEEDS. WE SHOULDN'T BE HALFHEARTED WITH SERVING GOD BECAUSE WE ARE PLOWING A PATH FOR OTHERS TO GROW! SOMEONE IS WATCHING AND DEPENDING ON YOU TO HANG ON TO YOUR FAITH. THEY WILL GROW BECAUSE OF THE GOOD DEEDS, PRAYERS, WORDS OF ENCOURAGEMENT, AND CONSISTENCY OF YOUR WALK WITH CHRIST! I DON'T CARE HOW HARD LIFE GETS, NEVER LOOK BACK, AND KEEP SOWING GOOD SEEDS BECAUSE SOMEONE YOU LOVE WILL REAP THE BENEFITS OF YOUR LABOR AND FAITHFULNESS SOMEWHERE DOWN THE LINE. YOUR SEEDS MATTER!

Family Assignment

RECALL AND SHARE A STORY WITH YOUR FAMILY ABOUT A GREAT SACRIFICE A FAMILY MEMBER OR RANDOM FRIEND MADE AND HOW THE RESULTS BLESSED YOU TREMENDOUSLY. IF THAT PERSON IS ALIVE, CALL THEM UP AND THANK THEM! THEY MAY NOT HAVE THE SLIGHTEST IDEA HOW THEIR SACRIFICE BLESSED YOUR LIFE!

HEALING ROOTS

I DO NOT KNOW OF ONE FAMILY THAT IS PERFECT OR FREE FROM TOXIC TRAITS. I CAN BOLDLY SAY THAT BECAUSE SATAN IS STILL EMPLOYED ON HIS JOB OF BEING EVIL, AND ONE OF HIS BIGGEST TARGETS IS FAMILIES. SATAN HATES A STRONG FAMILY UNIT. HE HATES IT WHEN BROTHERS AND SISTERS CAN GET ALONG. HE GETS NERVOUS WHEN HUSBANDS AND WIVES PRAY AND GROW TOGETHER. IT MAKES HIM ANGRY TO SEE CHILDREN HONORING THEIR PARENTS. THEREFORE, HE PLANTS SEEDS OF OFFENSE AND HURT AMONG FAMILY. ALSO, THERE ARE SOME FAMILIES AT WAR NOT ONLY AMONG THEMSELVES, BUT THEY HAVE GRUDGES AGAINST PEOPLE OUTSIDE OF THEIR FAMILY UNIT. GET THIS, MOST TIMES IT HAS NOTHING TO DO WITH THOSE WHO ARE STILL CARRYING THE "FAMILY GRUDGE CROSS." NOW WOULD BE A GOOD TIME TO UPROOT HATE, ANGER, AND OFFENSE (ESPECIALLY IN THE MIDST OF THIS CURRENT GLOBAL PANDEMIC) AMONG YOUR KIN. MANY FAMILIES FUNCTION DISABLED SIMPLY BECAUSE PEOPLE REFUSE TO FORGIVE AND HEAL. THERE IS AN OLD ADAGE THAT SAYS, "TIME HEALS ALL WOUNDS." THAT IS NOT TRUE. THERE ARE PLENTY OF PEOPLE WHO DIED AND WERE BURIED WITH OLD-FRESH WOUNDS. WHAT DO I MEAN BY OLD-FRESH? THE WOUNDS ARE OLD (TRANSFERRED FROM PAST GENERATIONS) BUT FRESH (PRESENTLY PAINFUL). THESE ARE THE ROOTS THAT SHOULD BE UNCOVERED (TALKED ABOUT), TREATED (SOAKED WITH LOVE AND FORGIVENESS), AND NURSED BACK TO HEALTH (HAVE THE TESTIMONY OF RECONCILIATION) (SCRIPTURE REFERENCE MATTHEW 5: 23-24). I HEAR YOU SAYING, "SHAE THAT'S NOT EVEN BIBLICAL," BUT I BEG TO DIFFER. DO YOU REMEMBER THE TWIN BROTHERS ESAU AND JACOB? THEY FELL OUT BADLY OVER BETRAYAL. THE SPIRIT OF BETRAYAL AND MANIPULATION WERE PASSED DOWN FROM THE PREVIOUS GENERATION. THINGS DIDN'T MEND UNTIL JACOB FACED HIS BROTHER ESAU (UNCOVERED THE WOUND) AND THEY TALKED, AND JACOB REPENTED (TREATED THE WOUND WITH LOVE AND FORGIVENESS) AND

THE RELATIONSHIP WAS NURSED BACK TO HEALTH (WE READ THE POWER OF
THEIR RECONCILIATION IN SCRIPTURES TODAY). SOME OF YOU READING THIS
HAVE LOST TRUE FRIENDS, LOVING FAMILY, AND ARE DETERMINED TO HOLD
YOUR GRUDGES LIKE A NEWBORN BABY. ENOUGH TIME HAS PASSED ALREADY,
AND TOMORROW IS NOT GUARANTEED. DON'T LET THE SUN GO DOWN
ANOTHER DAY WHILE YOU ARE ANGRY. HEALING IS A BENEFIT OF THE
KINGDOM, BUT YOU HAVE TO GO TO THE ROOT WHERE IT HURTS IN ORDER TO
BE MADE WHOLE. THE NEXT GENERATION DOES NOT HAVE TO BLEED IF YOU
CAUTERIZE THE ROOT!

Family Assignment

CALL UP AN OLD FRIEND OR FAMILY MEMBER THAT YOU DON'T LIKE HOW
THINGS ENDED. PRAY BEFORE YOU CALL. HAVE A PRODUCTIVE
CONVERSATION TO SEE IF YOU CAN COME TO A PLACE OF RECONCILIATION OR
AT LEAST CLOSURE. BE ACCOUNTABLE AND APOLOGIZE FOR YOUR PART OF THE
MISUNDERSTANDING. FORGIVE AND LET IT GO. PRESERVE THE ROOT!

TOXIC ROOTS

Killing the Little Foxes

FAMILY TOXICITY IS NOTHING NEW. ISSUES TRANSFER AND ARE PASSED DOWN THROUGH GENERATIONS. SOMETIMES THIS CAN EVEN BE LEARNED BEHAVIOR. TOXIC TRAITS SHOULD BE ADDRESSED AND STOPPED VERSUS BEING IGNORED AND GROWING. LET'S DO A QUICK BIBLE STUDY IF WE MAY. TURN (IN YOUR PAPER BIBLES) TO 1ST SAMUEL 15:1-9. PLEASE READ THE TEXT BECAUSE IF NOT, WHAT I'M ABOUT TO PARAPHRASE WILL NOT MAKE SENSE TO YOU. SAMUEL GAVE KING SAUL CLEAR CUT INSTRUCTIONS ON HOW TO DEFEAT HIS ENEMIES THE AMALEKITES. THERE WAS NO QUESTION ABOUT WHO AND WHAT ALL HE SHOULD KILL AND DESTROY. OK, KING SAUL LEAVES WITH THE INSTRUCTIONS IN MIND, BUT THE ROOT OF REBELLION IS IN HIS HEART. GUESS WHAT HE DOES? HE KILLS "SOME" OF THE LIVESTOCK BUT KEPT THE BEST-LOOKING ANIMALS FOR HIMSELF. HE ALSO SPARED THE LIFE OF THE AMALEKITE KING (THE HEAD OF THE ENEMY)! IN 2021 HE WOULD BE HAILED AS BRILLIANT (HE COULD EXECUTE THE PLAN), A BUSINESSMAN (BECAUSE HE REFUSED TO CUT PROFITABLE ASSETS AND THEY GO TO WASTE), AND ONE WHO DEMANDS RESPECT (BECAUSE HE KEPT HIS ENEMY ALIVE TO SEE HIS VICTORY)! CAN YOU IMAGINE FACEBOOK, TWITTER, AND INSTAGRAM GOING WILD HAILING KING SAUL AS THE MAN OF THE CENTURY? HERE IS THE PROBLEM WITH THAT CELEBRATORY MINDSET. HE COULD BE HAILED HONORABLE ON EARTH, BUT HE IS TOTALLY DISAPPROVED AND REJECTED IN HEAVEN (1ST SAMUEL 15: 11). PASTOR STAN SAYS THIS PHRASE OFTEN, "PARTIAL OBEDIENCE IS COMPLETE

DISOBEDIENCE IN THE EYES OF GOD". KING SAUL HAD A TOXIC TRAIT. HE REFUSED TO DESTROY IT! NOW, WHAT DOES THIS HAVE TO DO WITH YOUR FAMILY? THERE IS NOT A RAPIST OR CHILD MOLESTER IN EVERY FAMILY, BUT SOMETIMES IT'S THE SUBTLE THINGS AMONG FAMILY THAT CREATE TOXIC ENVIRONMENTS. NEGATIVITY, GOSSIP, LAZINESS, RIDICULE, RACISM, PREJUDICES, AND ABUSE COULD BE JUST AS TOXIC AS THE VILE STUFF THAT IS DEEMED UNACCEPTABLE. NONE OF IT IS BENEFICIAL FOR FAMILY GROWTH. YOU DO NOT HAVE TO CURSE AT YOUR CHILDREN AND CALL THEM NAMES TO GET THEIR ATTENTION. YOU DO NOT HAVE TO HAVE FIST AND CUSS FIGHTS IN YOUR MARRIAGE BEHIND CLOSED DOORS AND THEN GO TO CHURCH THE NEXT DAY AND SHOUT AS IF NOTHING HAPPENED. YOU DO NOT HAVE TO BE AN ALCOHOLIC OR DEAD-BEAT DAD SINCE YOUR DAD WAS NOT IN YOUR LIFE. YOU DO NOT HAVE TO BE BITTER AND MEAN TOWARDS MEN SIMPLY BECAUSE ONE BROKE YOUR HEART. YOU DON'T HAVE TO BE MEAN AT ALL! WHAT PURPOSE DOES IT SERVES TO HAVE AN ATTITUDE 24/7? ARE YOU APPROACHABLE OR DODGE-WORTHY (NOBODY WANTS TO DEAL WITH YOU BECAUSE OF YOUR ATTITUDE)? MAM/SIR YOU ARE A TREE, AND WHATEVER IS IN YOU WILL BRANCH OUT TO NOURISH THE FRUIT OF YOUR LOINS. WHAT ARE YOU FEEDING YOUR OFFSPRING? IS IT BENEFICIAL AND FULL OF SUBSTANCE, OR IS IT POISON THAT LEADS TO EMOTIONAL INSTABILITY AND DEATH? YOU GET TO CHOOSE WHAT GROWS IN YOUR LIFE. I ADMONISH YOU TO KILL ALL TOXICITY AND STOP IT FROM SPREADING ANY FURTHER! THESE TYPES OF BEHAVIORS SHOULD NOT BE PRESERVED. THEY SHOULD BE UTTERLY DESTROYED. GO TO THE SOURCE OF YOUR ISSUES. THE EXCUSE OF SAYING "WELL THAT'S HOW I WAS RAISED" OR "THAT'S ALL I KNOW" IS NOT GOOD ENOUGH. A PERSON HAS TO DECIDE TO DO BETTER AFTER THEY HAVE LEARNED BETTER. YOU HAVE TO TAKE INITIATIVE AND END THE TOXIC CYCLES.

YOU HAVE TO REFUSE TO ARGUE AND FIGHT. YOU HAVE TO DISCIPLINE YOUR LANGUAGE AND PUT AWAY NEGATIVITY AND HATEFUL SPEECH. IF YOU WANT YOUR SEED TO THRIVE AND BE HEALTHY, YOU HAVE TO FIRST CLEAN UP YOUR OWN ENVIRONMENT. IT CAN BE DONE, I PROMISE. HOW DO I KNOW? I AM A LIVING TESTIMONY. I WAKE UP DAILY CHOOSING TO DESTROY TOXIC ROOTS. YOU SHOULD TOO.

Family Assignment

TAKE SOME TIME TO IDENTIFY ANY TOXIC TRAITS THAT HAVE BEEN INHERITED WHETHER LEARNED OR TAUGHT. LIST THEM ONE BY ONE AND IDENTIFY THE SOURCE OF THE BEHAVIOR. WHERE DID YOU LEARN IT FROM? WHO DID YOU SEE PERFORM THIS ACT? WHO VIOLATED YOU? WHO ABUSED YOU? MAKE A SEPARATE LIST THAT SHOWS WHY YOU CAN NO LONGER AFFORD FOR THIS TO CONTINUE IN YOUR FAMILY TREE. MAKE A CONSCIOUS DECISION THAT WHATEVER YOU DISCOVER ENDS WITH YOU! REACH OUT TO A COUNSELOR IF THE ISSUES ARE DEEP ROOTED. IT IS SO BENEFICIAL TO GO FORWARD WITH ENDING THESE BEHAVIORS. THE HEALTH OF YOUR FUTURE GENERATIONS DEPENDS ON YOU! YOU CAN DO IT! KILL IT!

Chapter Notes and Thoughts

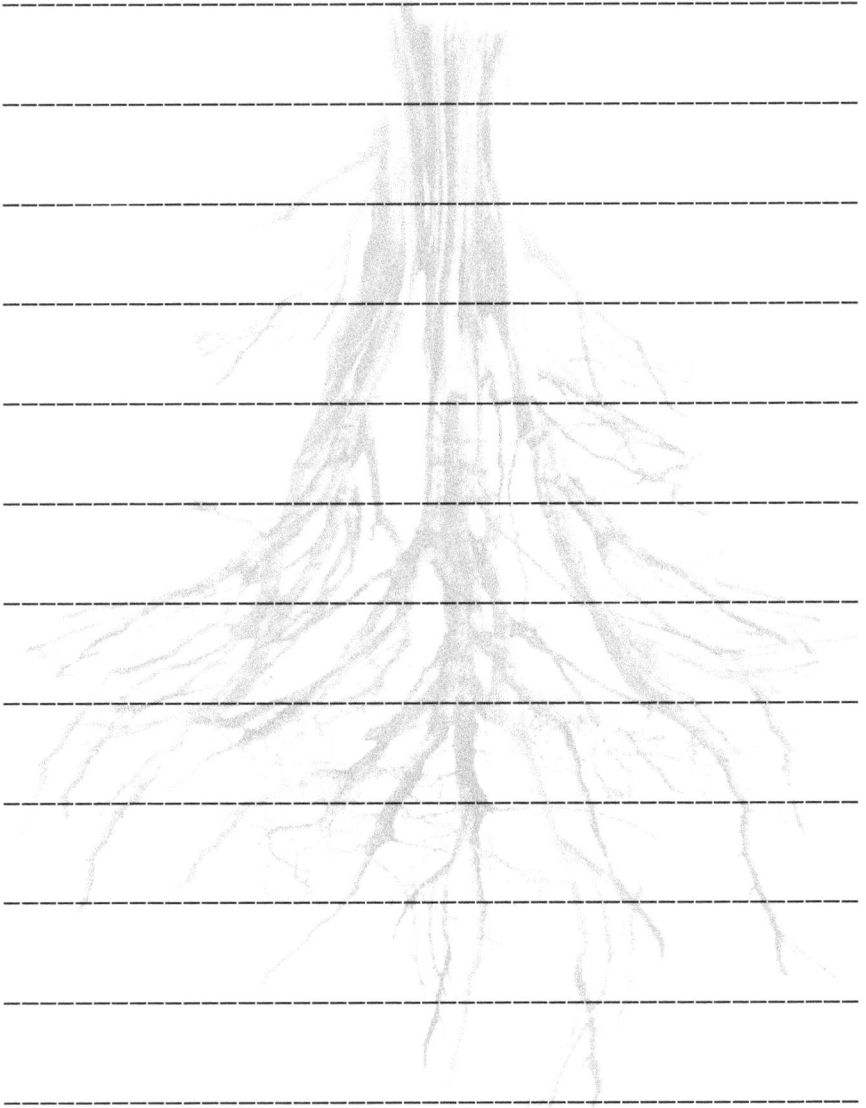

THE ROOT OF OFFENSE AND UNFORGIVENESS

THE ROOT OF OFFENSE IS A HARD ONE TO DIG UP SOMETIMES. IT IS EVEN HARD TO APPROACH SIMPLY BECAUSE IT FEELS IT HAS THE RIGHT TO BE PLACED RIGHT WHERE IT IS. IT WILL LET YOU KNOW REALLY QUICK WHERE TO GET OFF AND TO NOT BOTHER IT BECAUSE IT DOES NOT BOTHER THE REST (SO IT FEELS). HERE IS THE ISSUE WITH THIS ROOT. JUST LIKE WHEN ATHLETES STRATEGICALLY PLAY OFFENSE TO ADVANCE THE BALL DOWN THE COURT OR FIELD TO GAIN POINTS, THIS ROOT DOES THE SAME THING. IT ADVANCES INTO OTHER TERRITORIES OF A PERSON'S SPIRIT TO WHERE NOTHING IN THEIR LIFE IS APPROACHABLE. EVEN THE SIMPLEST THING CAN CAUSE A PROBLEM WITH THE PERSON WHO HOUSES THE ROOT OF OFFENSE. THIS ROOT HINDERS THE PERSON FROM PRODUCTIVE RELATIONSHIPS, OCCUPATIONS, ADVANCING IN MINISTRY, OR ANYTHING THAT LEADS TO ADVANCEMENT. THE OFFENDED ROOT CAUSES ONE TO BE STUCK AND LEAVES THEM IDOLIZING THEIR EMOTIONS. IT INTERTWINES WITH THE ROOT OF SELFISHNESS, UNFORGIVENESS, AND THE ROOT OF PRIDE. THIS ROOT IS NOT WORTH THE DAMAGE IT CAUSES. IF YOU HAVE THIS ROOT, ASK THE HOLY SPIRIT TO REVEAL THE PLACE WHERE IT IS BURIED AND ASK GOD TO HELP DESTROY IT BY HIS POWER! DON'T BE SURPRISED IF YOU FIND THAT THE ROOT OF OFFENCE IS ENTWINED WITH UNFORGIVENESS. LET'S DISCUSS UNFORGIVENESS! THIS IS A REALLY TOUGH ONE, BUT IT MUST BE ADDRESSED. WE MUST FORGIVE IN ORDER FOR OUR HEAVENLY FATHER TO FORGIVE US (MATTHEW 6:14), AND UNFORGIVENESS LEADS TO UNANSWERED PRAYER (MARK 11:25). THIS IS AN IMPORTANT SUBJECT BECAUSE PETER BROUGHT IT UP TO JESUS CONCERNING HOW MANY TIMES TO FORGIVE A PERSON. PETER THOUGHT THAT SEVEN TIMES WOULD BE SUFFICIENT, BUT JESUS ADDED EVEN MORE!

Jesus said to forgive a person seventy times seven (Matthew 18:22). Peter thought he was being generous based off the Rabbinic teaching of the day, but Jesus informs Peter (as well as the rest of us) that forgiveness is a continuous act. Even if we're done wrong multiple times in a day, we must forgive each time (Luke 17:1-4). This type of forgiveness does not require any extra amount of faith, but we do it because it's our duty as servants of Jesus (Luke 17:5-9). Always keep a forgiving heart so that bitterness won't take root and hinder your walk with Christ.

In conclusion, you cannot advance with either root in your life because at some point someone will step on them, and you in offense may turn around and abort your season! These are serious roots! Your next level may be at stake if you keep these roots around! Get rid of them because I sure ridded myself of mine!

Family Assignment

In order to combat the root of offense, forgiveness must be present and readily available for healing. The challenging part is that sometimes forgiveness has to be given even when it has not been requested or asked for. Identify sources of family friction against one another and maybe even others. Forgive and let the drama and grudges go. Free the next generation from fighting battles that were never theirs to fight to begin with. If you want to take something to your grave, let it be the fact that you learned how to forgive and let offences go!

THE SECRET ROOT

THIS ONE IS A SNEAKY ONE. I HAVE TO DISCUSS THIS ONE BECAUSE IT WILL DESTROY WHATEVER AND WHOEVER IS IN ITS PATH. THIS ROOT HAS NO RESPECTER OR PERSONS, AND IT WILL LIE SILENTLY FOR YEARS BUT LOUDLY TORTURE THE MIND OF ITS CARRIER. THIS IS THE 'ELEPHANT IN THE ROOM" A PERSON CAN BE AWARE OF, BUT NO ONE WANTS TO ADDRESS THE ISSUES AT HAND. I WILL TODAY. THIS ROOT STEMS FROM GENERATIONS BACK AND CAN BE TRACED AS FAR BACK AS IN THE BOOK OF GENESIS! THIS ROOT IS WHERE PERVERSION STEMS FROM. SOME OF THE PERVERSIONS ARE INCEST, MOLESTATION, RAPE, FAMILY INFIDELITY, AND CHILDREN BORN BUT NOT PROPERLY IDENTIFIED BY THE FATHER, BUT NO ONE TALKS ABOUT IT. THIS IS A SICK MENTALITY, AND THIS ROOT MUST BE STOPPED! FIRST OF ALL, IT IS NOT OKAY TO STAY SILENT IN REGARD TO ANY OF THESE PERVERSIONS. THE FACT THAT YOU DON'T WANT TO "STIR THE POT" IS NOT EVEN A REAL EXCUSE, ESPECIALLY IN 2021. DO YOU KNOW HOW MANY PEOPLE ARE SILENTLY HURTING BECAUSE THEY HAVE BEEN TOUCHED INAPPROPRIATELY AT THE HOMES OF FAMILY BY VARIOUS MEMBERS? DO YOU KNOW HOW MANY HALF SIBLINGS ARE IN THE EARTH, BUT NO ONE DARES TO SAY WHO THE CHILD'S REAL FATHER OR MOTHER IS? EVEN MORE UPSETTING, DO YOU KNOW THAT YOUNG GIRLS CAN'T EVEN DEVELOP INTO YOUNG LADIES, WHICH IS A NATURAL AND BEAUTIFUL THING, BUT YOU HAVE NASTY UNCLES AND COUSINS EYEING THEIR EVERY BUDDING FEATURE? OKAY, IT'S EVEN GETTING BAD WITH WOMEN LUSTING AFTER OUR YOUNG MEN! THIS IS A SLAVE MENTALITY. THIS HAS TO STOP! IT IS A SPIRIT, AND IF IT IS NOT CONFRONTED AND DEALT WITH, IT WILL CONTINUE TO SILENTLY GROW.

SINCE IT IS A SPIRIT, YOU HAVE TO CONFRONT IT IN THE SPIRIT. YOU HAVE TO ADDRESS THE SPIRIT OF PERVERSION AND CALL IT WHAT IT IS! IT IS A **nasty, foul, perverted spirit**. DON'T GET ME WRONG, PERVERSION IS RUNNING RAMPANT IN THE EARTH NOWADAYS ANYWAY, BUT IT DOES NOT HAVE TO RESIDE IN YOUR HOUSE. DEAL WITH IT!

FAMILY ASSIGNMENT

THIS ROOT CAN BE A TRICKY ONE TO DISMANTLE FOR THE SIMPLE FACT THAT SOMETIMES PEOPLE TEND TO DENY THAT IT EXISTS. THE ONLY WAY TO DEFEAT THIS ROOT IS THROUGH HONESTY. SECRETS WITHIN FAMILIES STUNT FAMILY HEALTH AND GROWTH. HONESTY HURTS, BUT IT ALSO HEALS. PRAY AND ASK GOD ON HOW TO HAVE AN OPEN AND HONEST CONVERSATION. WITH GOD AS YOUR GUIDE AND YOUR SPEECH SEASONED WITH LOVE AND THE HOLY SPIRIT, THINGS CAN GO BETTER THAN KEEPING SECRETS IN SILENCE.

Notes and Thoughts

_____

_____

_____

_____

_____

THE ROOT OF UNDERSTANDING

How well do you perceive and understand matters in life? There is a peace and level of Godly wisdom that accompany understanding. James 1:5 states, "If any of you lack wisdom, let him ask of God, that giveth to all men liberally and upbraideth not." I think for most of society we are great at expressing our points of view and emotions, but we are lacking in the understanding area. I would like to share an instance that happened sporadically during my nursing career. Please bear with me!

When I first began nursing at the age of 21, I was assigned a patient who it was apparent that he did not like people of color. This was not an assumption because he made it known verbally on more than one occasion that people of color were not welcome in his room. Well, this particular night, he had no choice because I was assigned, and he had no other choice than to receive care from me. I had this rotation for 3 consecutive nights. I'd go in and he'd be really rude, but here is the level of understanding that I possessed. I saw his age and quickly identified the era in which he was raised (1930s-1950s). Therefore, I understood that even though his actions were irritating and unfavorable (in my sight), I was there to be his nurse regardless of his beliefs. I was respectful and kind even when he wasn't. This guy was dying and rather quickly. Right before the shift ended of my last night with him, I passed him his bedtime pill cup and he grabbed my arm. I was startled at first, but the look in his eyes did not portray that he was intending harm. He just stared at my skin as he held my hand. His next response drew a well of tears from my eyes as his action drew tears from his as well. With a quivering voice he stated, "Gal, I don't mean to be mean, but I was raised this way." I placed my other hand on his and softly whispered, "Sir, I understand." He and I shared a moment that will go with me to my grave. I asked could I pray for him because it was not wise for him to close his eyes and face eternity with a heart full of hate.

I shared that story because in today's time, we tend to extend grace and love to those who look like us, are kin to us, or friends with us! The root of understanding lends a healing grace to those who are not in your defined circle. I had every right to complain about serving that man, but I offered grace through understanding. I may not agree with all of the calamity in the world today, but I do feel strongly about standing on knowledgeable ground. I do this because that's what Jesus did. He was positioned on a cross between two criminals. One could care less about Him, while the other briefly communicated to understand Him. Look what the root of understanding gained for the seeking criminal. He gained an instant trip to Paradise (Heaven) (Luke 23:43).

I would like to encourage you that if the seed of understanding is not in your character garden, please plant one today! You need it. Beautiful things can grow or sprout when it takes root. If Christ be in you, this seed is included in the redemption package you received! Why do I say that? I say that because Romans 5:8 proves when it was planted. If you understand that you need grace, then what makes you think that others are not worthy of receiving grace? Having an understanding is therapeutic in a crazy world. Plant it and watch it grow!

Family Assignment

Consider a situation that in hindsight you may have judged harshly without cause. Re-assess with the eyes of understanding. You may be surprised at what you see.

THE ROOT OF COMMUNITY

A few years ago, we were offered an opportunity to move to another state. It was a pretty sweet deal, and we were really tempted to make the move, but what kept us here was our community. We kept having the conversation of moving to a bigger city, but the perplexing situation was finding another school district as amazing as our current one. We turned down an exciting opportunity because we were already connected to amazing people. Sometimes, God will lead you to uproot your life in order to branch out in other places. However, there will be times where He wants you to bloom where you're planted. Sometimes the most precious jewels are already in your vicinity. Being involved in your community can lead to discoveries of hidden talents, meaningful relationships, and a lifetime of precious memories. Sometimes certain people can be the gift that God gave you to make your gift flourish. Honestly, we would dare not ignore the impact of our community even in our personal lives. Our children have been blessed with some amazing teachers and administrators, and their impact will continue to have a lasting effect and a permanent place in their lives.

With that being said, this root is priceless if cultivated correctly. Many challenges can come to a community, but genuine love should hold it together when tough circumstances arise. Choose your words wisely. If you have the choice to speak negatively or positively about someone in your community, take the opportunity to speak well. This root of community should be preserved, and you will be blessed by the fruit it bears.

<u>Family Assignment</u>

Take a moment of reflection and inventory of your community. Take note of what you love about it, and purposely pray about the things that you don't. At the end of the day, a community is better when it stands together.

Notes and Thoughts

ABOUT THE AUTHOR

SHALANDOR "SHAE" REEL- JOHNSON IS A RESIDENT OF HOUSTON, MS. SHE HAS DEDICATED MUCH OF HER ADULT LIFE TO NURSING AND SHE HAS WORKED IN NURSING FOR TWENTY YEARS AND COUNTING. SHE IS THE PROUD WIFE OF PASTOR STAN JOHNSON AND THE MOTHER OF THREE MULTI-TALENTED CHILDREN KIRK, KIRKLYN, AND LASARAH JOHNSON. SHAE HAS ALSO WORKED ALONGSIDE HER HUSBAND IN MINISTRY AS AN ORDAINED EVANGELIST SINCE 2007. SHE LOVES TO SING, TRAVEL, AND DO PHOTOGRAPHY ON THE SIDE. SHAE IS THE AUTHOR OF GOD IS POWERFUL AND EXTREMELY DISABLED.

Notes and Thoughts

FOLLOW US ON SOCIAL MEDIA

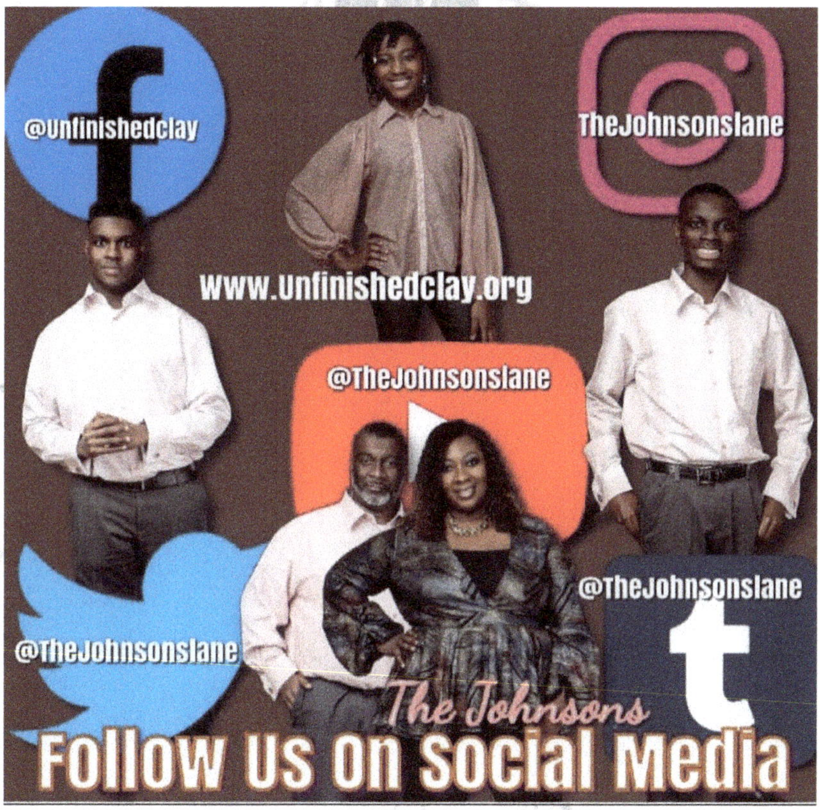

www.ingramcontent.com/pod-product-compliance
Lightning Source LLC
Chambersburg PA
CBHW050019090426
42734CB00021B/3335